IMPROVING YOUR
PRESENTATION
SKILLS

2

IMPROVING YOUR PRESENTATION SKILLS

A COMPLETE ACTION KIT

MICHAEL STEVENS

KOGAN
PAGE

To my parents, for caring,
and Peter, for understanding

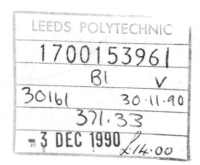
First published in Great Britain in 1987 by
Kogan Page Ltd, 120 Pentonville Road, London N1 9JN

Reprinted 1988, 1990

British Library Cataloguing in Publication Data
Stevens, Michael
    Improving you presentation skills: a complete action kit
    I.   Communication in management
    1.   Title
    658.4'038   HD30.3

    ISBN 1-85091-319-6

Printed and bound in Great Britain by Martin's of Berwick Ltd

Contents

Acknowledgements

Several people have contributed to the writing of this book, but in particular I would like to thank Jean Wadlow, Managing Director of Wadlow Grosvenor, for introducing me to the subject of presentation training; Derek Coltman, Education Director at the Institute of Directors, who, in a brief meeting, demonstrated the art of effective presentation; and Heather Hullah, formerly Manager of In-Company Services at BACIE, for her past guidance in writing this type of book.

ABOUT THIS BOOK

Getting your message across clearly and convincingly – whether in letters, interviews, speeches, reports, meetings, or through the media – is the single most effective way of achieving professional success. It can win business, enhance your reputation or simply make you more effective at doing your job.

This may sound easy. After all, we share our thoughts every day in conversation. But presenting information so that it will influence your audience in precisely the way you want requires careful planning. Reading this book will help you learn the basic skills and techniques involved in getting your message across effectively.

Learning by doing is an excellent way of improving your skills. Unfortunately, because of the high stakes, few of us can risk our professional reputations while practising our presentation skills. Each chapter of this book provides you with:

- **activities**
  to help you recognize your strengths and weaknesses as a communicator, and learn the skills and techniques needed to achieve results with your presentations, without risk of losing face, customers or money
- **guidelines**
  to compare with your work on the activities (there are usually no *right* or *wrong* answers)
- **key points**
  for every aspect of making presentations, as a checklist at the end of each chapter
- **signposts**
  to help you work through the book easily.

Occasionally you may be tempted to skip an activity, or even part of a chapter. If you are serious about improving your presentation skills, resist the temptation. The book has been structured to give you the most help in the least time.

For those who stick with it, the rewards are good. This book will help you become better at presenting information, adding to your confidence, prestige and career prospects.

INTRODUCTION

There are few situations at work where you would not benefit from knowing how to present information effectively. Sometimes the rewards can be unexpected and large.

What you can achieve

In common with many parts of the motor industry, the early 1980s were a lean time for one factory. Although employing only 300 people, it is part of one of Britain's largest chassis engineering groups. After two years of loss-making the factory manager, a production engineer by profession, took a realistic look at the factory's potential. In a report to the board of directors he recommended what he felt was the only realistic option – closure.

A management accountant was sent in to confirm this. After a thorough investigation he submitted his report, which concluded that with the correct management the factory could be making a profit within two years. That report persuaded the board of directors to give the factory another two years to return to profitability, and the accountant was given the job of justifying his belief – as factory manager.

Within two years the factory was making a profit, and the former accountant was rewarded with the job of managing the group's largest factory, employing 3,000 people. At the time it too was making a loss.

Again he produced a report, this time concluding that the factory could be made profitable within three years. The board were impressed and said, 'Do it!' The incentive was a seat on the board of a company which employs 8,000 people. Within two years the factory returned to profitability and he was guaranteed his directorship.

If you had to describe, step by step, how to write a report or plan any type of presentation to achieve such positive results, would you know what was involved?

How to achieve results

Whatever information you want to get across, and whatever your reasons, there are simple steps you can take to achieve the results you seek. This book gives you the opportunity to learn the skills and techniques involved. After reading it you will be able to:

- understand the importance of using a **structured approach** to preparing, rehearsing and delivering your presentations (Chapter 1)
- **analyse your audience** to find out what will make them listen, understand and accept your message (Chapter 2)
- **organize your message** so that it is clear and forceful (Chapter 3)
- **select appropriate aids** to increase the clarity and impact of your ideas (Chapter 4)
- **rehearse** a speech to ensure that you deliver it effectively (Chapter 5)
- **deliver a speech** in a dynamic way, to create interest and enthusiasm amongst your audience (Chapter 6)
- **write reports and letters** which are read and which achieve results (Chapter 7)
- **use meetings, conferences and interviews** to create a positive image for yourself (Chapter 8)
- **use the media** effectively to get your message across to a mass audience (Chapter 9)
- **assess your performance** as a communicator of ideas (Chapter 10), and if necessary
- **select training** in presentation skills and techniques which is appropriate to your needs (Directory).

SIGNPOST Whatever the type of presentation you are making, thorough preparation is vital. Chapter 1 explains why.

1 SO YOU WANT TO BE A BETTER PRESENTER!

Before you can learn new skills or improve those you have already, you need a reason for learning and an understanding of what is involved. This chapter will help you recognize

- **how much you know** about presenting information effectively
- **what is at stake** when you make presentations, and
- **how problems can arise** when you don't prepare carefully.

Do you know what is involved?

ACTIVITY

These questions cover some of the major skills and techniques needed to present information clearly and convincingly. Circle the number alongside your answer to each question.

What is one of the basic aims of a presentation?
- to entertain the audience   3
- to display your knowledge of the subject   4
- to get them thinking like you   ①

Which group of people in an audience is the most influential?
- those who are interested in attending   4
- those who will use the information you present   ②
- those who have the most power   6

If you had a choice, how long would you speak to have the best chance of getting your message across?
- ten minutes   ②
- thirty minutes   3
- one hour   5

Which of these methods would you use to avoid boring an audience with your presentation?
- make it entertaining   5
- make it relevant to them   ②
- use spectacular visual aids   3

Which is the best reason for using a visual aid?
- because the idea is dull without it   4
- because it gives another view of the idea   2
- because it is the best way to explain the idea   ①

When you are using visual aids which of these should you never do?
- introduce and explain it   4
- remain silent while the audience absorbs the information   ①
- ask for questions   2

When is the best time to do a final rewrite of your presentation?
- before rehearsals   4
- during rehearsals   1
- after rehearsal   ②

What would you recommend someone *not* to do during rehearsal?
- change the presentation   6
- practice in front of a live audience   ③
- learn the speech word for word   2

Which is most likely to help you make a convincing presentation?
- learning how to control the signs of your nervousness   ①
- learning how to relax   3
- learning not to worry   5

If some of your audience obviously aren't listening, do you
- carry on?   4
- say or do something to make them listen?   ②
- concentrate on those who are listening?   6

In a presentation, what is one of the best ways of making members of your audience feel involved in what you are saying?
- speaking loudly   4
- asking for their views   6
- looking at them   ①

For a technical report, which are the most important readers?
- the most senior   6
- those who can take action on the proposals   2
- those who will understand the technical content   4

What is one of the major advantages of presenting your ideas in a report rather than a speech?
- it can be more detailed   5
- you can choose your words more carefully   2
- your audience can read it in their own time   4

When writing a letter should you aim to achieve the same basic things as when making a speech or writing a report
- always?   1
- sometimes?   2
- never?   3

After making a speech, a question has been asked which you are unable to answer. Do you
- move on quickly to the next question?   4
- bluff and answer as best you can?   6
- explain that you don't have the information and ask if anyone in the audience can help?   1

You are being interviewed for a job you want, although you don't have the relevant experience. Do you
- stretch the truth convincingly?   5
- explain why you think you can do the job?   2
- avoid the subject of your experience?   3

When you ask a question during a conference, which of the following is most likely to boost your image?
- displaying your understanding and knowledge of the subject   5
- cleverly highlighting a flaw in the speaker's argument   6
- explaining your experience of the subject   1

In a radio interview, which would be most effective?
- making one point several times   2
- making several points once   3
- remaining flexible and playing it by ear   5

During a heated debate on television one of the other panel
members interrupts you mid-sentence. Do you
- let her finish and then continue?   3
- raise your voice slightly and continue?   1
- let her finish and then reply to her comment?   4

After making a presentation, which of the following would best
describe your feelings (be honest)?
- relief that it is over   3
- eagerness to know what effect it had   1
- worried that you may have made a fool of yourself   5

Add the numbers you have circled. Your total =

How effective do you think you are, or would be, at making a presentation (tick
one)?

        Good   Fair   Poor

Now read on and see if your assessment is realistic.

GUIDELINES This questionnaire isn't a foolproof way of assessing your abilities as a presenter, but it will give you an idea of how methodical you are, or would be, in making presentations, and your chances of always achieving the results you want.

Your score

65–100 If you are making presentations and achieving good results, the methods you use are probably unorthodox and your success may be more luck than judgement. Your score suggests that you don't know many of the techniques commonly accepted as the best way of getting a message across to an audience. You would benefit from learning these techniques and how to apply them.

35–65 You have a fairly good grasp of what is involved in presenting information effectively, but your ideas aren't consistent. By learning to be more methodical in your approach, you will be able to take advantage of all the techniques which help get a message across clearly and convincingly.

Below 35 Well done! You seem to know a lot about how to get a message across effectively. But knowing is not the same as doing, and you could still benefit from practice in applying your knowledge. Even if you make presentations that always give you the results you want, don't be complacent. The most successful presenters stay on top by constantly polishing their technique.

What is at stake?

Even if it's a routine activity for you, such as attending a meeting or writing a letter, failing to present information effectively can cause serious setbacks to your business or career.

Shortly after his appointment, a junior Government official learnt the hard way that it is wise never to be caught off-guard by the press.

A national survey of spending habits had shown that people in one region of the country relied more heavily on credit than others. Apparently unaware of the likely consequences, the official gave a personal assessment of the facts. Without thinking about how it might be interpreted, he explained that this was probably due to their inability to understand money matters.

This made the national news headlines, with people from all walks of life reacting violently to what they felt was an offensive comment aimed at reinforcing class distinction. Belief in his competence to do the job took a nosedive, and during the next six months he spent more time defending his statements than explaining them.

Competition is fierce in the telecommunications industry. In 1986 one of the country's leading suppliers submitted a tender for the installation of equipment worth £6 million. Twelve copies of a report were prepared and sent to executives in the client organization.

When the contract was awarded six months later, it was a competitor who won the business. Angry that their bid had failed, a regional director arranged a meeting with the client. Returning to his office red-faced, he had to explain to his bosses why they had lost this major contract.

The report contained a detailed analysis of the cost of the work, which was referred to continually in the main text. Unfortunately, four of the copies contained a set of figures which was quite different from that in the other eight, making nonsense of the report. The client realized that it must have been an administrative error – but who would pay £6 million for that level of efficiency? The company lost the business, and the manager responsible for compiling the report almost lost his job.

How to avoid disasters

The consequences of poor presentation skills are not always as dramatic as in these examples. But every time you make a presentation you may run similar risks if you fail to control the situation effectively.

There are basically four components in any presentation. The mnemonic AM/PM will help you remember them:

- your **audience** and the **medium** (speech, report, etc) through which you reach them (*AM*)
- you, the **presenter**, and your **message** (*PM*).

If you want to communicate effectively you must control each of these components.

ACTIVITY

Name two ways related to each, in which you could fail to achieve the results you want from a presentation.

audience	*medium*
1.	1.
2.	2.

presenter	*message*
1.	1.
2.	2.

GUIDELINES You may have chosen other examples, but these are some of the ways in which you can fail to control a presentation effectively:

Audience

- you didn't know why they were there and so failed to provide the information they really needed
- you bored them with too dull and too long a message
- you overestimated their knowledge of the subject and they couldn't understand what you were talking about.

Medium

- the convincing speech you prepared for your interview on the radio was useless when you discovered that you only had two minutes to get your ideas across
- the slides you planned to use turned up in the wrong order, confusing everyone, including yourself
- your eight page report read like an essay on poetry and the client couldn't figure out the conclusion you had drawn and the recommendations you were making.

Presenter

- you recited your speech word for word, making it sound flat and unconvincing
- stagefright got the better of you and you mumbled most of your message
- you didn't want to do the presentation and didn't seem very enthusiastic – so neither did your audience.

Message

- you weren't clear about the message you wanted to get across, so the audience had little chance of knowing either
- the ideas you introduced were difficult to understand, but you didn't explain them
- the examples you used to explain your ideas weren't relevant to your audience, so you lost their interest and your message lost its impact.

You can avoid problems like these by being methodical when you plan your presentations, so that you can control the outcome. There are three basic stages:

- finding out about your audience
- writing your presentation to suit the audience and the medium you are using
- delivering your message in a way that takes advantage of the medium.

The remaining chapters of this book provide a step-by-step guide to help you to do these things.

Chapters 2 to 6 are written from the general viewpoint of making a speech. The same basic techniques are recommended for preparing all types of presentation, with some modifications which are described in Chapters 7 to 9.

KEY POINTS

- take a realistic look at your strengths and weaknesses in making presentations
- recognize the importance of overcoming your weaknesses
- have confidence that you can control the outcome of a presentation.

SIGNPOST

Deciding what your audience needs from your presentation is the first step in achieving the results *you* want. You can learn how to do this by reading Chapter 2.

2 THE PEOPLE WHO MATTER

You must never take it for granted that because you have an audience they will listen to what you say. Even when they do listen, how can you be sure that they will understand and accept your message? They will need and expect different things from your presentation.

If you want to get your message across effectively you must express it in a way which appeals to your audience. This chapter shows you how to analyse your audience to find out what will make them **listen, understand and accept your message**. It involves answering these questions:

- who will be there?
- why are they coming?
- what do they want to hear?
- why might they stop listening?

ACTIVITY   What is the *one* thing that every presentation should aim to achieve?

GUIDELINES You may have found it difficult to answer this question because different types of presentation obviously seek to achieve different things. But whatever the mesage and whatever the medium, **the common aim of all presentations is to create some change in the audience,** eg:

- a technical report might aim to **convince** readers that an industrial accident was not due to cutting corners on the maintenance of machinery
- in a television interview you might be defending a policy decision by your organization, and will want your audience to **believe** that it's in their best interests
- at a meeting you may want to **persuade** colleagues that you are on the verge of a major breakthrough and that they should continue to fund your research.

It is important to remember that an audience, whatever its size, is a **collection of individuals** and not a faceless mass. Achieving the results you want depends on your knowledge of your audience. The more you know about them, the more control you can exert in making them listen, understand, and accept your message. It helps you decide *what* to say and *how* to say it.

Who will be there?

You may know precisely who will be at your presentation, but if not, try to find out. This can be difficult, particularly with a lay audience, but sources like the organizer, a meeting agenda or conference notes will help you.

 ACTIVITY What broad categories could you use to divide your audience when you don't know them personally?

This is a good way to start analysing your audience, dividing them into categories such as:

> male/female
> age
> lay members
> profession
> specialist area
> employer/employee
> clients and customers (existing and prospective)
> colleagues (superiors, equals, subordinates)
> competitors or rivals

When you don't know members of your audience personally, dividing them into categories will help you decide later how they are likely to feel about the subject of your presentation.

Why are they coming?

Knowing why people are attending your presentation will help you decide what they expect from you.

What general reasons might you have for attending a presentation?

GUIDELINES   Most people attend presentations for one or more of the following reasons:

a) to be entertained
b) attendance is compulsory
c) they are interested in the subject
d) they need information.

a) The 'joy riders'

For a variety of reasons, people sometimes go to presentations to be entertained. Although this should never be one of your primary aims in making a business presentation, you shouldn't ignore the opportunity to influence a wider audience.

b) The captive audience

I am excluding from this group people whose job it is to find out about your presentation. If attendance is compulsory you are at least guaranteed the size of your audience and you can usually find out exactly who will be attending. The major disadvantage is that you may have to work harder to keep them interested.

If most of your audience fall into these two groups you should think seriously about your reason for making the presentation. The aim of a presentation is to achieve results and neither of these groups is likely to help you directly to do that. The remaining two groups already have an interest in listening to what you say.

c) Those who want to know

Most audiences won't know exactly what they want to hear until you tell them. Few people analyse their motives for attending a presentation. They tend to think about it in broad terms of 'interest' or gathering 'useful' information. But they are there, like the next group, because they feel a 'need' to be there.

d) Those who need to know

This group is very influential. They intend to use the information you give them to achieve something; eg a rival might be looking for flaws in your argument to discredit you or block your progress.

Both of these groups may want information for a variety of reasons, eg:

- to help them make a decision
- to evaluate their options
- to pass on to other people, or
- to satisfy various 'psychological needs'.

The next step is to decide *what information* they want from you.

What do they want to hear?

If you can express your message in terms of what the audience want, they are more likely to listen and accept what you say.

For each of the following situations, write down the possible feelings of the audience.

situation	possible feelings
a meeting of senior company management with shop stewards to discuss redundancies	
a talk by a researcher at a professional conference about his recent discoveries	
a television interview with a leading politician about his decision to resign because of a personal vendetta against him	

GUIDELINES

In most situations you can identify the feelings which are likely to predominate in your audience, eg:

- the shop stewards may feel distrust, hostility, resentment or apprehension
- the researcher's audience may feel interest, curiosity or resentment
- the people watching the political interview may feel sympathy, apathy, curiosity or anger.

If you want to get the audience on your side, your presentation must include information appropriate to their particular range of feelings, eg:

- to satisfy their curiosity
- to meet their expectation of interest
- to give them a reason to trust rather than distrust you
- to allay concern, and so on.

In some situations you may want to use your presentation to **reinforce their feelings**, eg:

- their hostility towards a common enemy
- their anger about an injustice against you
- their distrust of a mutual rival's motives.

Using your category list of people in the audience you can find out how they are likely to feel about your presentation by answering such questions as:

- does it have special significance for them?
- do they want to achieve something for themselves or for others by being there?
- will they gain or lose by my proposals, and how?
- do they have stereotyped views?
- what is their personal opinion of me?
- do they need my help in making a decision?
- what are their powers to take action on my proposals?
- do our views coincide or differ, and by how much?
- do they have a particular axe to grind?

ACTIVITY

Imagine an audience listening to a speaker at a public enquiry on proposed sites for a nuclear power station. List four things about members of the audience which might influence how they feel about the speaker's message:

1.

2.

3.

4.

GUIDELINES In this type of situation, individual views will be shaped by a mixture of knowledge, beliefs and emotions. Some of the main factors determining how they feel will be:

- their occupation (eg the mining, coal and nuclear industries, or an industry dependent on power)
- their knowledge of the nuclear industry and recent events concerning the industry (eg accidents)
- their feelings about nuclear weapons
- the location of their home and family
- their upbringing and social background
- their political views.

The more questions you ask about your audience, even if they provide similar answers, the easier it will be to present your message in a way which appeals to them.

Why might they stop listening?

If you are giving people the information you think they need, why should they not listen to what you say? Up to now we've considered only what they need to hear, but your message may include information they don't want to hear. The solution is to avoid saying things in a way which has a negative effect.

 List the reasons why you would mentally 'switch off' from what was being said at a presentation.

Whatever the type of presentation, members of the audience tend to switch off when:

- they are bored, either because it's not relevant to them, or it's relevant but not interesting
- it doesn't give them the information they expect or need
- they don't understand what is being said
- they are distracted, or
- they are threatened or offended by what is said.

The first two of these problems can be overcome by deciding what information the audience wants from you, as described earlier. The remaining three require special consideration:

a) What will they understand?
b) What might distract them?
c) What would they find threatening or offensive?

Will they understand?

ACTIVITY   List the possible reasons why an audience might not understand you.

GUIDELINES

The problems are fairly obvious. Your audience may not understand you if:

- they cannot hear what you are saying because your voice is too quiet or because you don't speak clearly
- you use jargon, technical terms or other unfamiliar words
- you don't explain difficult concepts or ideas.

These problems can be avoided easily by answering more questions about the situation, such as:

- what is their level of understanding (which may include educational, social and professional factors)?
- what do they know about the subject?
- does the size of the venue mean that I need to use a microphone?

Avoiding distractions

After making the effort to find out what information will interest your audience, you must avoid anything that might distract them from listening.

Even at this early stage you should consider when and where the presentation will take place. This can have an important influence on how your audience reacts to your presentation.

ACTIVITY

What distractions could be created by the time and place of your presentation?

GUIDELINES Again, the problems are fairly obvious, but they can be easily overlooked. For example, the audience will be distracted from listening if:

- there is background noise (eg traffic, noisy ventilation, people passing)
- there are interruptions
- the seating is uncomfortable
- the room is too cold, or too hot and stuffy
- they are eager to go to lunch, or to go home
- the lighting is too dim or too bright
- they can't see or hear you clearly.

All of these factors should be considered at an early stage of your preparation.

What is offensive or threatening?

Most people will be antagonized if you say something which they find even mildly offensive or threatening. You can destroy weeks of work in an instant if you fail to consider this point.

Avoiding being offensive to your audience is fairly straightforward. Do not use language which may offend them, and make sure that you are aware of what are likely to be 'sensitive' subjects, so that you can phrase your comments carefully. You need to answer such questions as

- what is their national or regional origin?
- what is their sex?
- what is their age?
- do they have sympathies with any minority group?
- do they have strong political or religious beliefs?
- do they have prejudices about any specific subject?

Avoiding posing threats to your audience is a more difficult problem. The natural reaction to a threat is either to try to overcome it, perhaps by destroying the presenter's argument, or to ignore both the threat and the rest of the presenter's message. If you trigger either of these reactions you immediately make your task difficult, if not impossible.

What type of things might pose a threat to an audience?

GUIDELINES   Whether it is real or not, any implied threat in your presentation will cause an unwanted reaction in your audience. For example, this can happen if your ideas:

- threaten their security, or that of their family, friends, or colleagues
- infringe their area of operation
- compete for money or space
- detract from their prestige or position
- damage their reputation, or that of colleagues or their organization
- challenge strongly held beliefs (eg political, religious or moral).

Turn these points into questions and you can identify ideas which might threaten your audience. These ideas can still be included in your presentation, provided they are introduced carefully. You can learn how to do this in Chapter 3.

The time spent on this activity is well worth the effort. It provides you with a tool that you can use whenever you need to make a presentation. Write a comprehensive checklist of questions which you should ask yourself about the type of audience who might attend one of your presentations (ie all the aspects covered in this chapter).

KEY POINTS

- who will be in your audience?
- what information will they want from you?
- how will they feel about what you have to say?
- are these feelings an advantage or disadvantage in getting your message across?

SIGNPOST

You are now ready to take advantage of what you have discovered about your audience when you write your presentation. This is the subject of Chapter 3.

3 PUTTING YOUR IDEAS TOGETHER

Talking in conservation is so natural that we rarely have to stop and decide how to convey a message. In a presentation you must *plan carefully what to say and how to say it* to achieve the results you want.

After analysing your audience you know what they will listen to, understand and accept. You know broadly what you want to achieve by your presentation. This chapter shows you how to tie the two together to write a presentation which is clear and convincing. Whatever ideas you want to get across, it will help you to:

- **Write objectives** to act as guidelines for writing your presentation
- **Get all your ideas on paper** to ensure that you cover all the important points
- **Structure your message** so that it is easy to follow
- **Support your ideas** so that they are relevant to your audience, clear and have impact
- **Prepare an outline** of your presentation which you can use to rehearse, and
- **Choose an effective title.**

Writing objectives

Objectives are statements of what you want to achieve by making your presentation. They serve at least three important functions:

- they are a constant reminder of what you need to achieve in writing the presentation
- they help reduce a complicated message into manageable chunks, making it easier for you to write and your audience to follow and understand
- they provide a way of measuring the success of your presentation.

Answering the question, 'Why am I making this presentation?' will provide your objectives, but to be useful they need to be worded in a certain way.

ACTIVITY

Decide whether or not each of the following objectives is effectively worded, and say why:

stated objective	is it effective ... why?
1. to tell students how to make effective presentations	
2. to prove to colleagues that more expenditure, not less, will increase efficiency	
3. to explain how the new management structure will benefit employees	
4. to win sales	

GUIDELINES Objectives should reflect how you want your audience to have changed after hearing your presentation. This can be measured in terms of action or understanding. Only two of the examples given are stated in this way:

1. no – because it doesn't state the audience response you want to achieve

2. yes – because the desired audience response is clear – acceptance of the idea. It is also measurable

3. no – for the same reason as 1

4. yes – because the audience response is implicit, ie they will buy the product or service.

State your objectives in *dynamic terms*, using words such as convince, believe, persuade, understand, agree, do, say, or prove, *not passively* with words like tell, show, explain or help.

Even if you have one outcome in mind, this may involve more than one objective, eg:

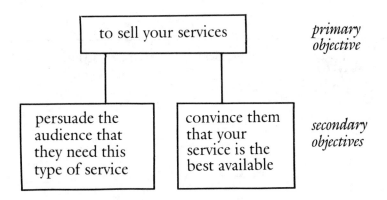

The more specifically you can state the changes you want to achieve in your audience, the more effective you can make your presentation. This may involve writing further objectives when you have decided on the structure of your presentation.

> *Check how well you have stated your objectives*
>
> - is my intention clear?
> - does it state what audience response I want?
> - is that response measurable?

Rewrite any objectives which fail one of these tests. You can check them again by reading them aloud to someone and asking for their comments. Extra time spent testing your objectives now will improve your chances of success and save you time and effort later.

Throughout the rest of your writing task, keep a note of your objectives in front of you.

Getting all your ideas on paper

If you are short of time, or confident that you know your subject well, you may be tempted to start drafting your speech or report as soon as you've written your objectives, without first putting all your ideas on paper. This would be a mistake.

ACTIVITY

What problems could it create for you?

GUIDELINES

Even if you feel you have a good grasp of all aspects of a subject, trying to put them on paper in their finished form can be a slow, frustrating and ineffective way of writing a presentation. You are asking your brain to do three things at once, each requiring different thinking skills.

Trying to recall the information, put it in a logical order, and state it clearly all in one step can cloud your thinking. You risk:

- choosing a 'storyline' or structure which is not the simplest or most effective way of getting your ideas across
- excluding important information because you momentarily forget, or because it doesn't fit into the storyline you have chosen
- not meeting the needs of your audience because you have failed to include them in the writing process
- not choosing the most important points.

The technique recommended helps you avoid these problems and provides a list of ideas for the next stage:

- make sure you will not be interrupted
- write down all your thoughts on the subject, quickly and randomly
- don't stop to explain, link or justify ideas
- let the ideas flow and keep writing
- when you've exhausted the subject, put your notes aside.

Structuring your message

The next step is to put your ideas together in a short and simple message.

| Keep |
| It |
| Short and |
| Simple |

KISS is a well-known acronym for making effective presentations:

- short because people concentrate best in short bursts
- simple because the easier it is to follow, the more your audience will understand.

▼ **ACTIVITY** Imagine you are making a speech with the objective of enabling your audience to do more work in less time. Here are some of the notes you might have at this stage. Draw six arrows between the two columns to show how they are related. One example is given.

audience needs	*subject notes*
	obligations
	thinking time
	delegation
to understand where	making time
their time goes	time-logs
	unfinished work
	meetings
to be able to	routine activities
save time	lack of planning
	self-discipline
	controlling time
to be reassured	interruptions
they are not	travelling
alone in thinking	no time to think
that there aren't	laziness
enough hours in	deciding priorities
the day	setting time limits
	fatigue
	scheduling
to do more in	diary
less time	overtime
	emergencies
	efficiency
	time-wasting

Now choose four main points or categories from the subject notes which are of major interest to the audience.

1.

2.

3.

4.

GUIDELINES   What you have done is to start giving a structure to your presentation which:

- will help you fulfil the needs you identified in your audience
- breaks down a complex subject into a simple sequence of ideas.

Depending on how you view the subject, you may have chosen these as your main points:

1. making time
2. time-wasting
3. controlling time
4. lack of time.

For any presentation you should use only three or four main points. This helps you get the ideas clear in your mind as well as helping your audience follow what you say. If you have more than three or four points it suggests that you haven't chosen the broadest categories, perhaps mistaking explanation (eg interruptions) for a main point (time-wasting).

Once you've decided on your main points, list each of them on separate 5in × 7in index cards. This will help you in the following stages.

The next step is to select three or four subheadings from your notes for each main point, and add these to the relevant cards. You will then have a basic structure for your presentation.

For example:

time-wasting	*controlling time*
interruptions	deciding priorities
laziness	scheduling
lack of planning	self-discipline

making time	*lack of time*
delegation	unfinished work
travelling	no time to think
setting time limits	overtime

The final step is to decide the best order for presenting your main points. Usually there will be a 'natural' order, which seems the most logical way of explaining your subject. This may be the statement of a problem, followed by the description of a solution, eg:

the problem	*the solution*
lack of time	making time
time-wasting	controlling time

This type of structure is very common in the commercial, technical and scientific worlds, and there are many variations, eg asking a question and answering it, or highlighting a need and fulfilling it. Other types of order may be determined by importance or size, or when events are related in time, or by cause and effect. If there is a 'natural' order, use it. Your audience will find it easier to follow.

Supporting your ideas

Now you have to decide how to get these points across in a way which will:

- keep your audience listening, by sparking interest and enthusiasm
- help them understand, while giving your message impact
- if necessary, persuade your audience.

ACTIVITY

List five methods you could use to express your ideas so that you achieve these things, eg analogy.

1.

2.

3.

4.

5.

These are some of the more common methods you can use to help you get your ideas across effectively:

analogy	facts
anecdote	humour
anticlimax	metaphor
curiosity	narrative
definition	opinion
description	questions
emotion	quotations
exaggeration	repetition
example	statistics
explanation	understatement

Two other ways of supporting your ideas are discussed in later chapters. You can learn about:

- **visual and other aids** in Chapter 4, although they should be included in your message at this stage of preparation
- using your **voice and body** to help get your message across in Chapter 5.

Using any of these methods effectively relies on the information you obtained by analysing your audience. Some examples follow of how they can be used.

Keeping them listening

Audiences easily become bored and distracted, so you must express your ideas in a way that will make them listen.

Give two examples of how you could make your audience listen by the way you express an idea.

1.

2.

Anything that grabs their attention will make an audience listen. For example, you could:

- appeal to their curiosity, eg 'I'm going to tell you how you can do twice as much in half the time, without exerting yourself'
- tell them an anecdote, eg 'I remember as a schoolboy trying to trade with my parents – cleaning the car, tidying my room, even my pocket money – just so that I could stay up to watch a late-night boxing match. We all learn very early in life where the balance of power lies in supply and demand'

Explaining with impact

Although it may be simple to express an idea in terms which are easily understood, that method may not have impact, and vice versa. You should try to combine both explanation and impact, particularly if they are major points in your presentation.

Give one example of an effective way of getting each of these ideas across:

1. company expertise in a given field

2. the importance of the American space programme.

GUIDELINES

Provided it's expressed in terms your audience know and understand, you can use any method to give an idea impact, eg:

1. Instead of explaining the professional background of your company executives, you could quote a statistic, eg 'Our senior management have 2,000 years' experience in this area' (followed by an explanation that you mean collectively!)

2. Give an example which has implications for the audience, eg 'Without the Apollo missions your desktop micros might still fill half a room and cost more than your annual wage bill.'

Persuading your audience

Persuasion is not the same as manipulation. Getting your audience to accept your ideas, even if they are resolutely opposed to them, is a process of helping them see your ideas in a positive way. You can do this by:

- logical argument, presenting one or both sides, or
- satisfying needs or desires.

Here are some guidelines for using these methods.

Logical argument

From your audience analysis you should be aware of any likely opposition. Choosing carefully how you express your ideas can help you overcome this opposition.

ACTIVITY

Imagine you are telling the company salesforce about a proposal to increase their number by 20 per cent and reduce the size of individual sales areas, all with the aim of boosting profits. The salesmen naturally feel their commission is threatened. What method could you use to help overcome their opposition?

A logical argument must be based soundly on facts. In this situation you could present the facts in various ways, eg:

- quote statistical evidence to show that smaller sales areas will yield the same turnover (and commission) as the current-sized areas
- give an example of projected sales in one of the newly defined areas
- describe a parallel situation in which the salesmen benefited as well as the company.

Deciding whether to present just your side of the argument or to incorporate answers to the counter-argument depends on who is in your audience:

one side	both sides
when most are in favour	when most are opposed
subordinates rely on you for guidance	superiors will want the full picture
when they have to make a decision on the spot	if the counter-argument has or is going to be made known

If you choose to present one side of an argument you still need to prepare notes on the counter-argument. This will equip you to answer any questions from your audience when you make your speech.

Motivating them to accept

Dangling the carrot can be an effective way of persuading your audience, provided the carrot is real. Audience analysis will tell you what needs and desires motivate your audience. If you have a carrot which appeals to them, you can use it to persuade.

Imagine you are making a takeover bid for another company and you are appealing to its shareholders. What needs or desires might they have, and how could you appeal to them?

GUIDELINES

There are many possibilities. Depending on the situation, you could:

- appeal to greed, with an offer they can't refuse
- guarantee their independence, by confirming that there will be no interference in the company if the takeover bid is successful
- appeal to their sense of adventure, if yours is a new company with big ideas.

Other needs and desires you can use to persuade include:

ambition	power	reward	self-respect	recognition
security	approval	belonging	loyalty	pride

The motivation technique needs to be used with caution, because in some situations it may be ineffective and can even antagonize your audience. For example, your superiors might think you arrogant if you claim to know what is in their best interests. It is also a more subtle method of persuasion than logical argument and may not work if there is a strong counter-argument.

Check how effectively you have explained your ideas

- is it the most effective available?
- is it strictly relevant to my message and my audience?
- is it clearly stated?
- is it easy to understand?
- is it accurate and reliable?

If your answer to every question is yes, you should note the methods you will use alongside the appropriate points on your index cards.

Outlining your presentation

You now have a list of all the points you want to cover in your presentation and notes on how you will explain them to your audience. The process of outlining ties these two together into a single storyline, and provides a script you can use to rehearse.

Like any good story, presentations need a beginning, middle and end.

ACTIVITY

What should the following parts of a presentation do?

your introduction

your conclusion

GUIDELINES

The answer to this question lies in the old maxim: 'Tell them what you're going to tell them, tell them, then tell them what you've told them.'

Your *introduction* should:

- get audience attention and focus it on your presentation
- give them a taste of what is to come
- tell them the contents and structure of your presentation.

Your *conclusion* should:

- review what you've said with a summary, or an example which ties everything together (*never* introduce new points)
- be memorable
- state or imply what you expect your audience to do, believe, know, etc. as a result of your presentation.

At any type of presentation, the peak of concentration for most people in the audience is over after the first minute or so, with an increase in interest when they realize the end is near. Using your introduction to preview your message and your conclusion as a review makes the best of this aspect of human nature.

The best way of **creating an outline** is to look at each of your index cards in turn and, on separate pieces of paper, write one sentence for each point it contains. There are two guidelines you should follow:

- use language that your audience will understand
- link successive points in a way that tells the audience how they are related.

language they can understand	relating successive points
use:	*use:*
commonly used words	firstly,
simple verb tenses	as a result,
good grammar	this has led to, finally
sentences of about 15–20 words	summaries between main points
	if the subject is complex
avoid:	*avoid:*
long and uncommon words	repeated use of next,
jargon and technical terms	now, and so, also,
clichés	hence, and therefore
acronyms without explanation	
double meanings	
vague words like excessive and somewhat	

Because your introduction and conclusion serve a very important function, you should word them to have a precise effect on your audience.

Your outline is an ideal script to use for rehearsal. Notes to use when you deliver your speech are best prepared at the time so that you can incorporate any last-minute alterations.

Choosing an effective title

The first contact the audience have with your presentation is usually its title. First impressions are important. A good title should give your audience an exciting glimpse of what is to come and crystallize their thoughts on the subject, eg:

- Writing for effect
- Microcircuitry for macro profits
- Learning the easy way
- The pain of bankruptcy

Choosing a title is best left until near the end of your preparation because it should reflect the way you have organized your message. An effective title should:

- be brief (no more than four words)
- arouse audience interest
- tell them what your presentation is about
- be meaningful in its own right
- help integrate your presentation.

KEY POINTS

- write down how you want to influence your audience
- put all your ideas about the subject on paper
- choose three or four main points which interest your audience, and three or four secondary points for each one
- decide how to express these clearly and with impact
- write one sentence to explain each point
- make your introduction a preview of your presentation, and your conclusion a review
- give it a short meaningful title

SIGNPOST This chapter has shown you how to prepare an outline of your presentation, which may involve:

- selecting appropriate aids to help you get your message across (Chapter 4)

and from which you can:

- rehearse your presentation (Chapter 5).

4 MORE FOOD FOR THE EYES AND EARS

Sometimes words alone are not the most effective way of getting an idea across.

> The sales director of a security company had chosen to talk to a group of property managers from large retail chains in one of the company's ground floor offices. The curtains had been purposely closed. After welcoming the visitors, he began to introduce his talk but was suddenly interrupted by a thundering noise outside one of the windows.
>
> Walking over, he opened the curtains to reveal two men wielding sledgehammers at a large picture window. After about 15 seconds, having made no impression on the window, the two men put down the sledgehammers and walked away.
>
> The property managers looked amused and the sales director, apologizing for the interruption, continued his talk: 'You see gentleman, I do understand one of the problems you face. Fortunately, my company has the answer – a cheap, unbreakable substitute for plate glass'.

This is an example of one of the many types of 'aid' (including visual aids) which you can use to help you get your message across to an audience. This chapter will help you:

- recognize the **features of a good aid**
- become familiar with the **range available**
- select the **most effective** aid for the job
- learn **how to use them**.

What is a good aid?

The proper use of aids is to achieve something in your presentation that you can't do as effectively with words alone. They are only *a means to an end*, for instance to clarify an idea, or prove a point. A good aid is one which does this efficiently.

It is easy to fall into the trap of letting aids become the main feature of your presentation – writing it to suit the aids you want to use, or those available – but *the idea must always come first*. Even in advertising and design, where a storyboard or graphics may be an essential ingredient of a presentation, they are still only a means of explaining ideas.

Visual aids form the largest group. As well as the obvious, like slides and overhead transparencies, they include anything involving a visual image, such as the men attacking the window with sledgehammers.

ACTIVITY   What properties do visual images have that could help you get your message across in a presentation? It may help if you think of the ways in which information is presented visually, eg photographs, drawings and film.

GUIDELINES

The value of presenting information in a visual form depends on the idea and the situation, but there is a wide range of possible advantages, eg:

- it provides a refreshing change for the audience from just listening, and can grab their attention
- the audience can absorb information in a way and at a rate which suits them – if they don't grasp what you say, their chance of understanding is lost
- it is easier to understand complex information, eg relationships, procedures, and summaries, when it is presented visually
- pictures can stimulate the imagination more easily than words, increasing audience involvement
- they can trigger strong emotional responses and generate a particular mood among the audience
- 'worth a thousand words', they can save you time on explaining ideas
- information presented visually is remembered for a longer time

So there are clearly benefits in using aids. But there are also disadvantages which can make them less effective and even outweigh the benefits.

ACTIVITY

List the main drawbacks of using aids in a presentation.

GUIDELINES

When they are used for the wrong reasons or used badly, *all* aids have drawbacks. For example, they can:

- distract the audience from your message
- distract you from your purpose, by having to write, draw, operate equipment, and so on
- mislead the audience if they are not appropriate
- confuse the audience if they are not well designed
- unnecessarily add to the complexity of your presentation.

To avoid these problems, any aid you use in a presentation must be:

- appropriate to the idea and represent it accurately
- the best method available to get the idea across
- easy to understand
- used efficiently during the presentation.

What methods are available?

Almost any device that helps you achieve your objectives can be used as an aid. The most common ones are:

slides	overhead projector
audio tape	chalkboard
film and video	flipchart
maps	handouts
storyboards	graphs
displays or exhibits	demonstrations
an audience plant	props

Each of these has qualities which makes it suitable for supporting ideas in specific ways, eg:

- *props* can provide an unusual and striking introduction to an idea, or reinforce a point, eg the presenter wearing a bowler hat and explaining; 'This hat once deflected a falling brick and saved me from a long stay in hospital. If you don't have a bowler, it might be a good idea if you joined our private health care plan'

- *an audience plant* (where you have prearranged the cooperation of someone in the audience) is an effective way of separating two sides of an argument, eg by raising objections which you answer, or leading your presentation in a new direction by asking you a question.

ACTIVITY

Write down one way in which you could use each of the following aids:

aid   *possible uses*

slides

flipcharts

overhead projector

sound recording

handouts

demonstrations

GUIDELINES The variety of uses is enormous and you will have probably written down different ideas, but each gives a specific range of possibilities, eg:

aid	*possible uses*
slides	examples of before and after; pictures with strong human interest to generate a specific mood
flipcharts	drawing a flowchart to illustrate the stages in your presentation, adding to it as you go along, and then using it to summarize at the end
overhead projector	a series of overlays to show the development of an idea or procedure, or events in time; to show copies of documents or drawings made on a photocopier
sound recording	a message from an expert addressing your audience specifically; sound effects
handouts	samples of a product; statistics and other data
demonstrations	to show how efficiently a piece of equipment does its job; let the audience use it to see how easy it is to operate

A good aid adds to the effectiveness of your presentation. Deciding which to use, if any, should be done with as much care as you take in writing your presentation.

Which is the best aid for the job?

As an integral part of your presentation, aids should be selected during the writing process, when you realise that certain information is difficult to get across effectively using just words. But remember, they are only a means to an end. There *must* be a clear reason for using aids. If there is, you need to answer three questions:

- what type of help or support do I need to get the information across effectively?
- which is the best aid to provide that support?
- what is the most effective design for the aid I've chosen?

What type of support?

It is usually quite obvious from the nature of the information you want to get across, which type of support it needs. For example, you may want to:

- **explain** a concept, or the consequences of an event
- **reinforce** key points, radical ideas or proposals
- **clarify** complex data, relationships or procedures
- **define** a situation, or the scope of a problem
- **prove** a radical statement, or a conclusion
- **generate a mood** amongst the audience to make them more receptive to a particular idea.

Although it is possible to select an aid for the job without going through this process, it is a valuable first step. For example, if you wanted to highlight the world famine problem there would be a number of possibilities, including:

- defining it with statistics on food shortages or mortality rates
- explaining the consequences of malnutrition
- clarifying the causes of regional food shortages.
- generating a particular mood by showing the extent of Western food stores alongside the suffering of children in the Third World.

Analysing the situation in this way makes you aware of all the possibilities. Deciding which is the most effective type of support is a matter of personal choice, and will depend on the central theme of your presentation.

For example, a fund-raiser for famine relief might want to generate sympathy for the plight of Third World children, or guilt about 'food mountains' in the Western world, while a representative of a pharmaceuticals company might be more inclined to concentrate on the consequences of malnutrition.

Which is the most effective aid?

When you are analysing the situation and listing the possible types of support you could use, a particular type of aid to do the job effectively will often spring to mind. Each has a range of uses for which it is best suited.

ACTIVITY

This will give you some practice in selecting aids for a specific purpose. What aids would you use, and how would you use them in the following situations?

situation   *aid*

showing that, in arriving at your
conclusion, you have considered the
counter-argument

proving your track record in solving
corporate financial problems

explaining how you can deliver
goods within 24 hours of receiving
the order

showing how you pieced together
the solution to a problem

GUIDELINES   There is no limit to the number of ways you can use aids in a presentation, provided they are appropriate to the situation, eg:

situation	*aid*
showing that, in arriving at your conclusion, you have considered the counter-argument	an audience plant to raise points in the counter-argument; a telephone ringing on stage – an imaginary caller raising a point
proving your track record in solving corporate financial problems	personal testimony from executives in the relevant companies; a hand-out showing the profit and loss accounts before and after your help
explaining how you can deliver goods within 24 hours of receiving the order	a map on which you draw your distribution network while explaining how it works; film or video of your order-processing and despatch departments
showing how you pieced together the solution to a problem	drawing its parts on a flipchart or overhead transparancy to show how they are related

The most unusual use of an aid can sometimes be the most effective, particularly when your audience regularly attends presentations. Something new will stick in their minds.

Another factor to consider in deciding what type of aid to use is the different impact on your audience of pre-prepared aids (eg slides and displays) and those created during your presentation (written, drawn, and staged). Pre-prepared aids which are well-produced can add prestige to a presentation and boost audience confidence in your authority to speak on the subject. An aid produced on-the-spot helps you involve the audience and, because they've seen it created, they are more likely to accept the information.

> Once you've selected the type of aid you want to use, before developing it any further, check that:
>
> - it is suitable for the size of your audience and the venue for your presentation, eg passing your only sample around an audience of 400 people is impractical; so is a demonstration of a small hand tool in a large auditorium
>
> - if equipment or other facilities are required (or an audience plant), they will be available for your presentation
>
> - if the aid has to be created, eg a slide or film, the necessary skills and time are available for the work.

If you are satisfied that you can use the aid you have chosen, the next step is to design it to be as effective as possible.

Designing your aid

Even if you intend to use aids which are already available, such as slides, photographs or film, you must check that they are well-designed. A poorly-produced video shown in the middle of an otherwise excellent presentation can instantly destroy any enthusiasm your audience had for your ideas.

The same is true of information you intend to write or draw during the presentation. The design of every aid must be either planned or checked to ensure that it serves its purpose as efficiently as possible.

ACTIVITY

Figure 4.1 is an example of a poorly-designed visual aid. List the main features of what you consider is a well-designed visual aid.

features of a good visual aid:

the presenter's message is conveyed through words, images, structure, order, emphasis and gesture ...	but there can be a communication barrier created by lack of explanation, distractions, disinterest, misinterpretation, and poor articulation ...	and the audience has needs too – for specific information, understanding, self-respect, involvement, recognition and security

Figure 4.1   Example of a poorly designed visual aid

GUIDELINES   The design of visual aids should make it easy to recognize and understand the information they contain. So they need to be:

- simple, with details large enough to be seen by the most distant member of the audience
- uncluttered and clean-looking, with blank spaces so that details stand out, and bold lines to separate their parts
- as visual as possible, with key words rather than sentences and a minimum of numbers and symbols.

The basic information in the previous visual aid is shown more effectively in Figure 4.2.

The details could be either explained verbally or shown as additional aids. It is better to use several simple illustrations than to risk confusing your audience by cramming everything into one picture

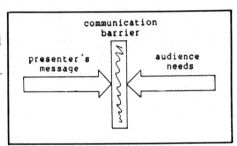

Figure 4.2   Example of an effective visual aid

The same principles govern the design of all aids. If you intend to write or draw information during your presentation, eg on a flipchart, you should decide exactly how you will present the information so that it will be seen clearly and understood.

If you are using props or 'stunts', don't embellish them with unnecessary activity. Keep them as simple as possible and they will have more impact.

If you are using slides, film, video or a soundtrack from an outside source, preview them so that you know they are of good quality and are exactly what you want.

If you are using handouts, make sure they are effective, eg printed information should be well laid-out (see Chapter 7), and samples should be of the best quality.

Following these guidelines will help you produce aids which have the best chance of achieving the effects you want, provided you use them properly.

How to use aids

The drawbacks of using aids were mentioned earlier.

One of the major problems is that they can interrupt the flow of a presentation, and disrupt the rapport you have built up with your audience. Another is that they make your presentation more complicated, eg by having to draw or operate equipment.

ACTIVITY

Write a list of guidelines which would help someone to avoid these problems, whether they were using pre-prepared aids or creating them on-the-spot.

GUIDELINES
To use aids effectively you should:

- maintain contact with your audience - face them frequently and re-establish eye contact; don't stand silently for too long, unless there's a soundtrack. Introduce and briefly explain your aids
- if you are using equipment, make sure it is available and working on the day, and that you know how to operate it
- make sure you have all your aids with you on the day, slides are in the right order, and so on
- if there is a visual element, make sure it is shown long enough for everyone to understand, but not so long as to be confused with later ideas or to provide a distraction
- if you are writing or drawing
  - do it on a clean surface,
  - make it large enough for all to see,
  - make it simple and legible,
  - write or draw quickly
- don't hand out material just before your presentation. If people must read it before, send it out in advance, otherwise hand it out at the relevant point in your presentation.

Selected carefully, designed well and used properly, aids will help you get your message across clearly and convincingly.

KEY POINTS
- only use aids when they are the best way to get information across
- select aids appropriate to the information
- use your imagination for the best results
- make them clear and easy to understand
- don't let them come between you and the audience.

SIGNPOST
You should always rehearse using your aids, following the guidelines given above, when you rehearse your speech. This is the subject of Chapter 5.

5 THE PRACTICE RUN

To think of rehearsal simply as practice is to forget that it is your last chance to perfect your presentation. Anyone who neglects this stage of preparation – and many do – risks wasting their time making a presentation. Whatever your reason for having to speak, this chapter will help you to:

- understand the importance of rehearsal and what it involves
- learn how to assess your rehearsal
- ensure your message is effective
- improve your delivery technique.

Rehearsal gives you the confidence to deliver your message with sincerity and conviction.

How to rehearse

Don't leave your rehearsal until the last minute – it can undermine your confidence. Rehearsing properly takes time and involves:

- learning the 'storyline' or sequence of ideas you will be presenting
- practising using your voice and body to get them across effectively
- checking that your message and your presentation technique are effective.

It can be tempting to learn a speech word for word, so that you can recite it without making a mistake. This can sound unconvincing, as if you are reading from a script. A presentation should sound spontaneous. The best way to do this is to learn the storyline during rehearsal and choose the words to tell the story when you are delivering your speech.

ACTIVITY | There are some exceptions to this rule. What parts of a presentation are best learned word for word?

GUIDELINES

In stressful situations it can be difficult to put words together in precisely the way you want. Some parts of your presentation have been written to fulfil a very important role and these can be committed to memory:

- your introduction
- factual information, such as statistics, anecdotes and quotations
- your conclusion.

Your outline is an ideal rehearsal script. As well as containing all your ideas and phrases to link them, it will help you remember to use simple language that your audience can understand. Keep reading your outline until you become totally familiar with every aspect of your message, including the aids you will be using. Use a slower speed than you would in conversation, as if you were telling a story to an audience.

Some people like to rehearse piecemeal, running through small parts of their presentation during quiet moments in their daily routine. Others like to restrict it to 'full dress' rehearsals. Whatever method you choose, you should always have at least two complete rehearsals, including any aids you are using. The purpose is to be able to deliver your presentation using only notes to trigger your memory.

Even when you are not due to make a formal presentation, you can practise using your voice and gestures effectively in regular self-coaching sessions. Being able to present information effectively is a valuable asset at any time.

How to assess your rehearsal

During rehearsal you need some form of feedback to tell you how effectively you are getting your ideas across. There are basically five sources of feedback:

1. Running through the presentation **in your mind** will tell you if you can remember the storyline and how you want to explain each idea. You can do this anywhere, at any time.

2. Rehearsing **aloud** gives you the feeling of what it will be like hearing yourself speak to an audience.

Most people like to start with method 1 or 2 to gain confidence. The options then are:

3. Recording rehearsals on **audio tape** will let you know how you will sound to your audience.

4. Asking one or more people to act as a **mock audience** will help you get an impartial opinion of how you look and sound. If possible, this should be someone with a knowledge of the presentation subject. This is a particularly good method for checking that your message is effective. It is also the only way to rehearse fully a presentation where there will be an exchange of ideas between yourself and someone else.

5. Recording rehearsals on **video tape** is an excellent way to find out how you look and sound. This method is used by many organizations offering training in presentation skills. The advantage is that *you* can assess your performance and see the improvement achieved by practice. A mirror is misleading and is a poor substitute. If you have the facilities, video tape is the best aid to rehearsal.

Is your message effective?

This is your last opportunity to make major changes in the content of your presentation. The best source of feedback is a mock audience with knowledge of the subject and who are willing to give you an honest assessment.

Write a list of questions a mock audience would need to answer in analysing the effectiveness of your message.

GUIDELINES A mock audience should look for all the things you have tried to achieve while preparing your presentation, such as:

- does the introduction grab attention?
- does it tell you what is to come?
- is there a clear central theme?
- is it easy to follow?
- are the ideas well explained?
- is it interesting?
- is the choice of words right for the audience?
- is the information given used appropriately?
- is it accurate?
- does he seem to know what he's talking about?
- are the aids clear, relevant and effective?
- does it lead to the right conclusion?
- does the conclusion tie the whole thing together?
- does the speech run for the correct time?

You can add to this list and give it to your mock audience to help them assess your message. Once you have their opinion you can decide if it is necessary to change it in any way. It may need to be shortened, the ideas rearranged, more explanation given, material deleted, and so on. After making changes you should always repeat this evaluation until you are satisfied that you have got it right.

Improving your delivery technique

An effective delivery technique uses the voice and body to help get a message across.

ACTIVITY   If you were watching a video recording of your rehearsal, what questions would you ask yourself about your delivery technique?

GUIDELINES

Assessing your delivery technique involves answering such questions as:

- does my voice sound clear, confident and relaxed?
- does it convey feeling and meaning?
- do I appear enthusiastic about my message?
- am I sincere and convincing?
- do I have any distracting mannerisms?
- do I look 'presentable'?
- do I look confident and relaxed?
- is my pronunciation and articulation good?
- am I competent at using my aids?
- do they interrupt the flow of ideas?
- do I look at everyone in my imaginary audience, or fix my gaze?

Improving your delivery technique involves:

- ensuring that your voice, posture, gestures and general appearance add to the effectiveness of your words
- learning to control nervousness
- practising using your aids and any necessary equipment
- learning to watch for the audience response.

Listening to yourself

Whatever type of voice you have, it is your most effective tool for bringing your presentation to life. It can keep your audience spellbound, or put them to sleep. It can make your ideas sound new and exciting, or dull and boring. Learn to use it effectively and it will help you achieve your objectives.

People with strong **regional accents** sometimes panic at the thought of speaking in public. They think the accent makes their voice sound unattractive or difficult to understand. This is wrong. Accents often provide a refreshing change for an audience and even the broadest accents can usually be understood if the speaker articulates properly. Always use your natural voice.

If you listen to drama or short stories on the radio you can get an idea of how well the voice alone can convey subtle meaning. You want to achieve the same effect in your presentation.

ACTIVITY

Select a passage of about ten lines from a book and practise reading it aloud until you are satisfied that you are conveying its full meaning. Then make a recording and listen for the ways in which your voice varies and write down how each affects the meaning of what you say.

GUIDELINES

There are basically four ways of varying your voice. Here are some examples of how they can help to convey meaning:

- **speed**: slowing your speed can give emphasis to a statement, while speaking quickly gives a sense of urgency or excitement, provided you still articulate properly
- **volume**: raising the volume can highlight parts of a statement; a sudden drop in volume can grab attention
- **pitch**: in general, you should start sentences low and end higher. *Varying* pitch is important because it gives 'colour' to the voice. Continually high can be mistaken for nervousness; continually low makes you sound tired or depressed
- **pause**: pausing before an important statement heightens expectation and grabs attention. It also gives the audience time to digest what you have just said. But a pause of more than three or four seconds may sound as if you are lost for words.

However, listening to the way you sound is more important than following general guidelines, because there are many variations. You should practise using your voice to reflect enthusiasm for your message and to give your ideas meaning and impact.

Sometimes you may have to deliver your speech word for word from a script, eg if your comments will be put on record, or if there are legal implications. You should rehearse to achieve the same effect as with a speech from notes. Read it until you are confident that you know what it means and can reflect that in your delivery. Mark the places where you will pause, speak with greater emphasis, and so on, and keep rehearsing until you know exactly how you will convey the message.

Looking at yourself

You are the most valuable visual aid in a presentation. Your posture, gestures and general appearance have a powerful influence on what your audience think of you and your message.

ACTIVITY What words first come to mind to describe people with the following general appearance?

1. Slouched, frequent shrugs of the shoulders, weak and incomplete gestures, looking around aimlessly.

2. Stiffly upright, chin raised, chest out, staring intently at the audience, quick forceful gestures.

3. Upright yet relaxed, smiling, flowing gestures, gradually looking at all the people in the audience.

4. Fidgety, pacing up and down, frowning, indecisive gestures, avoiding looking at the audience.

GUIDELINES

How you view people is a personal matter, but you may have chosen words like:

1. careless, sloppy, shy
2. overconfident, arrogant, overbearing
3. friendly, trustworthy, believable
4. untrustworthy, secretive, uncertain.

Your posture, gestures, facial expressions and eye-contact with the audience reflect your feelings about yourself, your audience and your message. You must use them to create a positive image, appearing friendly and believable.

If you concentrate on getting your message across with its full meaning, gestures will come naturally. Gestures with the hands are especially powerful; since you want audience attention to be on your face, try to keep them above waist level.

The larger the audience, the larger the gestures need to be, but avoid deliberate, repetitive and irrelevant gestures – they don't look natural and can mislead your audience. Watch out for nervous habits, like playing with glasses, scratching your head or playing with the lobe of your ear – they are a distraction.

ACTIVITY

Give two reasons why taking care over your general appearance is important in a presentation.

1.

2.

First impressions stick, and the first thing your audience will notice is your general appearance. They may take it as a reflection of:

- your attitude towards them, your work and your organization, or
- the style and efficiency of your organization or department.

Create an image of caring about your appearance, but be yourself. Personal style is a reflection of your personality, so don't try to alter it just to suit the occasion.

Being well turned-out also makes you feel more confident, and it avoids distracting the audience with a crooked tie, ill-fitting clothes, and so on.

It is important that you feel comfortable and confident in these clothes. If necessary, rehearse while wearing them. You should decide well beforehand what you will wear. Putting on a few extra pounds could make you look untidy in your old standby.

There are special considerations about clothing when you appear on television, which are discussed in Chapter 9.

Controlling nervousness

Although you may not feel very nervous at the rehearsal stage, it is never too early to consider the problems that it can cause. For example, if the audience detect nervousness – by a quivering voice, stumbling over words, or unsteady movements – it may be interpreted as a sign that:

- you are unsure of yourself
- you are unsure of your facts
- you are lying, or
- you don't believe what you are saying.

Nervousness gets in the way of delivering your message convincingly. Ways of controlling it and using nervous energy to help you get your message accross with enthusiasm are discussed in Chapter 6.

Watching your audience

To get a message across effectively to an audience you have to watch their reactions to what you are saying. If they're not listening, you must do or say something to encourage them to listen. If you sense that they haven't understood or don't believe you, you must respond to these feelings.

It is difficult to rehearse how you will respond to an as yet invisible audience, but you can practise two aspects of your contact with the audience:

- maintaining eye-contact
- observing their behaviour.

When you rehearse, make a deliberate effort to scan all parts of the room, as if you're looking directly at individuals in your audience. When you are in a group of people talking, practise making eye-contact with each of them in turn, and watch how people react when someone is speaking to them. Learn to recognize different facial expressions, gestures and body movements, and what they mean. This will help you when you face a live audience.

'Reading' your audience and responding to them is discussed in detail in Chapter 6.

Preparing notes

Although your outline provides an ideal script for rehearsal, using it to deliver your speech can have the same effect as learning it word for word. The advantages of delivering from notes are that:

- choosing words spontaneously to explain your ideas sounds more natural, and is more believable and convincing
- you can remain flexible to respond to your audience
- it helps you become 'involved' in your message.

When you are satisfied that you have got your message right and know it, you can condense your outline into brief notes. These will fit on to small, unobtrusive cards, which you can number in sequence and refer to during your presentation to jog your memory.

ACTIVITY

What should your delivery notes contain?

GUIDELINES

The notes should contain:
- key words or phrases to help you recall each step of your message and the relevant support material
- cues for when to use aids
- the full text of any information you will have to write, draw or quote.

Some people like to use concise sentences, but the fewer words the better. Graphics can also be used, eg miniature visual aids as cues, or flowcharts to show a sequence of ideas. Use what works best for you.

Rehearsing for the unexpected

There are many situations where you may have to make 'off-the-cuff' comments on a particular subject, eg being asked unexpectedly to give a short talk, or answering questions. You can practise how to handle these situations effectively.

ACTIVITY

Get a friend or colleague to select a topic at random, which you both know well, and either:

- ask you to talk for a specific time on the subject (perhaps two or three minutes), or
- ask you questions on the subject, which you must answer as briefly and clearly as possible.

GUIDELINES

An impromptu talk or speech should not be a rambling collection of unrelated ideas. It should be organized like a prepared speech, as discussed in Chapter 3. Guidelines for answering questions in a variety of situations are given in Chapters 6 to 9.

KEY POINTS

- learn the 'story line', not the words of the story
- check that your message is effective – if not, rewrite it until it is
- practice using your voice and body to give your ideas meaning and impact
- condense your presentation outline into brief notes on delivery.

SIGNPOST

When you are confident that you know your message inside out and can deliver it effectively, your next step is 'Doing it for Real' (Chapter 6).

If your rehearsal hasn't gone smoothly, you may need to backtrack to earlier stages of preparation discussed in Chapters 2, 3 and 4.

6 DOING IT FOR REAL

Even after carefully planning and rehearsing a presentation, many people are worried by the thought that something will go wrong on the day. Fear is the presenter's worst enemy: fear of forgetting what you intended to say, of making a fool of yourself, and fear that the audience won't show any response to what you say.

Confidence in being able to spark enthusiasm in your audience and keep them interested is the key to successful delivery. This chapter will help you to:

- **take the stand confidently** by
  - preventing last-minute hitches, and
  - using 'stagefright' to your advantage
- **keep your audience involved** by
  - projecting your energy and enthusiasm, and
  - reading and responding to your audience
- **create a lasting impression** by
  - concluding with an emphatic statement, and
  - fielding questions effectively.

Preventing last-minute hitches

Executive air-travellers have been known to lose their luggage *en route* to important meetings and arrive minus clean shirt, well-pressed suit and, most disastrously, their presentation notes. Even if yours is taking place in the office next door, last-minute hitches can ruin a well-prepared presentation.

ACTIVITY

List eight of the things you would check on the day to ensure that your presentation stands the best chance of success.

1.   5.

2.   6.

3.   7.

4.   8.

GUIDELINES

Barring the building being razed to the ground by fire or similar unforeseeable circumstances, most things that could detract from your presentation can be eliminated by making a final check, eg:

- is all the equipment you require in position and working? Are spares — like a bulb for the slide projector – readily available?
- will the seating arrangement give your audience good visibility?
- does the lighting and temperature provide a comfortable environment?
- does the audience know exactly what time to be there?
- is there anything that might distract them – charts from a previous speaker, unused equipment, noise?
- if you are not the only speaker, do you know when it will be your turn to speak?
- is there anything that could make you late arriving?
- do you have everything you need for personal comfort – glasses, pills for headaches or hay fever, water for a dry throat, handkerchief for a running nose?
- do you look presentable – hair, teeth, zips, buttons, tie, shoes?
- do you have your notes (and a duplicate?) and in the correct order?
- do you have all your visual aids and other aids or props, and in the right order?
- have there been any last-minute developments – national news, or in-house policy – decisions which affect your speech? Are you prepared for them?

Checking all the possibilities will add to your confidence when the time comes to speak.

Using stagefright to your advantage

Stagefright can be a major problem for some people.

> The chairmen of two major British companies suffered a similar problem. Despite their professional success, they lacked confidence in speaking to large audiences. One always fainted shortly after taking the stand; the other stumbled through his speech almost incoherently. After training, both are now competent speakers, having learnt to control their fear of the situation.

Professional actors worry if they *don't* feel nervous before a performance. They know that the symptons of stagefright – butterflies, sweaty palms, trembling – reflect the high level of nervous energy they need to give a convincing performance.

 ACTIVITY
What physical signs do you show when you are very excited?

GUIDELINES The physical signs of excitement and stagefright are often the same. In both situations there is a high level of adrenalin in the blood, which prepares the body to exert extra energy. Until that energy is used it causes the 'symptoms' of stagefright.

Some people perform best when they are relaxed. If you are one of those people, there are exercises you can learn to help you relax. They are not covered in this book, but many of the organizations listed in the Directory cover this in their training. However, there are some simple steps you can take to minimize nervousness:

- **preparation** gives you confidence in your message and being able to deliver it effectively
- **belief in what you are saying** is the best way to overcome the fear of failure, or of looking foolish. Think of it as contributring to what you most want to achieve – approval, promotion, recognition, acceptance, or whatever
- **looking your best** helps you believe in yourself, increasing your self-confidence
- **forcing yourself to look calm** will help you stay calm. Make your gestures and body movements smooth and steady, try to keep your voice level and your breathing even.

Probably the greatest fear people have of speaking in public is 'drying up' or losing their train of thought. You can minimize the chances of this happening by using your finger as a marker on your notes. If it does happen, keep calm. Panic is contagious, so don't let your audience see that you are concerned. Look at your notes, pause to collect your thoughts and then pick up where you left off. It's better to pause, and even repeat yourself, rather than fumble. Never apologize.

Being totally relaxed can be a disadvantage though, if it robs you of vitality. It is far better to think of the signs of nervousness as an indication that your body is charged with energy, and use it to deliver your message. You may still feel weak at the knees and jumpy, but your audience is unlikely to notice. All they will see is a dynamic presenter.

A word of warning: It is unwise to drink alcohol to give you Dutch courage. It can cloud your thinking, impair your articulation and make you sluggish in reacting to your audience.

Projecting energy and enthusiasm

Mood is infectious. If you don't show enthusiasm over your message, neither will your audience. And if it looks 'staged', like poor acting, it will be unconvincing. You want your audience to feel involved, as if they were watching a good film. If they don't, they'll switch off before the end.

The only way you can achieve these things is to reflect your own involvement and belief in your message through your voice, posture and gestures. If you believe strongly in your message, the appropriate movements and intonation will come naturally.

First impressions are important. From the moment your audience can see you, look alert. When you stand to speak, take a couple of deep breaths, smile, acknowledge any introduction you have been given, and then immediately establish eye-contact with your audience. Concentrate on them, not the situation.

When you refer to your notes, look up and immediately re-establish eye-contact. Throughout your presentation, keep scanning your audience, exchanging glances with every member in turn. This is the best way to make them feel involved and maintain their interest.

Reading and reacting to your audience

When we are in conversation, we are constantly aware of the other person's reaction to what we are saying. Often unconsciously, we are looking for signs that we're getting through and being understood.

Every member of your audience merits the same attention. You need to know how they are reacting to what you say, so that you can make them listen when they're not listening, help them understand when they're confused, and so on.

ACTIVITY

What are the following audience reactions most likely to mean?

audience reaction	*likely meaning*
crossing arms and legs	
looking away	
shaking head	
leaning forward	
a quizzical look	
nodding	

GUIDELINES Watching people's feet, hands, facial expression, eyes and body movements will give you a fairly clear idea of what they might be feeling, eg:

audience reaction	*likely meaning*
crossing arms and legs	disagreement or feeling defensive, unless they're cold
looking away	distracted or disinterested
shaking head	disagreement or disapproval
leaning forward	interest, or unable to hear you clearly
a quizzical look	confused, don't understand, bored or tired
nodding	agreement or approval

These things may seem fairly obvious, but you should learn to recognize the signals and be ready to respond to the feelings they reflect. It will help you keep your audience listening and ensure that they understand.

If they look confused, perhaps you need to give more explanation or slow down. Ask a question to see if they understand. If there's a sudden change in their behaviour, could it be something you've just said? If they are disinterested or distracted, get their attention by pausing, asking a question, or using a visual aid to change pace.

Remain flexible. Be ready to adapt to your audience. And just because some people are listening and look interested, don't ignore them. Their enthusiasm can fire interest in others, so reinforce it by maintaining eye-contact with them.

Occasionally you may come across a person who has studied body language and uses that knowledge to confuse their rivals. This is most likely among skilled negotiators and salesmen, and you should be aware of the possibility.

Ending with impact

Your concluding statement may be the last contact you have with your audience, so it is vital that you leave them with a lasting impression. Look directly at your audience (you should know your conclusion word for word), speak slowly and deliberately, raising your voice to give it special emphasis. Your audience will sense that you are coming to the end and their concentration will automatically increase.

Fielding questions effectively

Even if the occasion of your presentation makes it unlikely that you will have to answer questions, it is wise to be prepared. The way you answer will affect the way your audience remembers the whole of your presentation.

When you were preparing your presentation you will have thought of likely questions and either:

- incorporated answers to them in your presentation, or
- prepared to answer them 'off-the-cuff'.

The first of these options is preferable, otherwise the audience will begin to concentrate on the 'unanswered questions' instead of your message. The only exception is when you have chosen to present one side of an argument. However, even if you've tried to cover all possible questions, you should be prepared for the unexpected.

ACTIVITY

Apart from wanting information, what reasons might your audience have for asking you questions?

GUIDELINES Questions which are not an appeal for information are asked to satisfy various needs, some of which you may have identified when analysing your audience, eg:

- to gain attention
- to display their knowledge
- to gain approval
- to inform you
- to relieve their boredom
- to lead you on to another subject, or away from one
- to raise their own concerns
- to disrupt your speech.

Knowing why people are asking questions helps you give answers which satisfy them.

Avoid asking your audience for questions during your speech, unless you want to check that they understand what you've said. If they interrupt you with a question, stop to answer it and then return to your speech as soon as possible. Although you will lose the continuity of ideas, leaving a question unanswered until the end of your speech will sound like evasion and may distract the audience from listening.

ACTIVITY In general terms, how would you respond to the following types of questions:

type of question	*how you would respond*
several questions in one	
one which includes incorrect information	
hostile	
rambling	
argumentative	
asking you to make a commitment	

GUIDELINES   The way you answer depends on the specific question and the way it was asked, but the following ways are effective:

type of question	how you would respond
several questions in one	ask what the main question is, and answer that
one which includes incorrect information	correct it, and then answer if it's still necessary
hostile	express understanding of the reason they feel as they do, but explain why you have said what they're reacting against
rambling	interrupt and ask what their question is
argumentative	answer in a way which reinforces what you've already said
asking you to make a commitment	don't make a promise you can't keep. If necessary, briefly explain why

Here are some **general guidelines** to help you answer questions:

- listen carefully to the question
- look at the questioner and try to decide from their manner and tone of voice why they are asking
- draw them out further if necessary
- repeat the question in your own words to ensure that you understand and everyone else has heard
- if it is a complex question, divide it into parts and state what each is before you answer
- relate your answers to points you have made in your speech. Don't raise new points
- answer briefly, keeping to the point
- if your answer must be more than a few sentences, give it structure – an introduction, middle and conclusion
- don't try to put questioners down, or ridicule them. Answer reasonably
- if you don't have the information to answer a question, say so, and ask if anyone in the audience can help
- don't argue under any circumstances.

Answering questions efficiently in this way will satisfy the questioner and create a good impression among the rest of the audience.

KEY POINTS
- check for last-minute hitches
- mood is infectious – use your nervous energy to project a dynamic image
- watch and respond to every member of your audience
- leave them with a lasting impression by giving your conclusion extra impact and answering any questions effectively.

SIGNPOST
As soon as possible after making your speech, assess your performance by reading Chapter 10.

7 PUTTING IT IN WRITING

When you are talking to an audience face-to-face you can sense how they are reacting and change your delivery technique to ensure that your message is getting across. **Letters and reports** are different. They don't have a live presenter to animate the ideas. You rely totally on their appearance, structure and content to make the audience read, understand and accept your message.

Letters and reports can also be reread, copied, circulated, and kept for future reference. So they are semi-permanent ambassadors reflecting an image of you and your organization.

This chapter will help you learn how to write letters and reports which:

- encourage people to read them
- are easy to follow and understand
- create the right impression
- achieve the results you want.

Reports

Reports can be divided broadly into two types:

- short reports of up to about 10 pages
- major reports which may run to 100 pages or more.

Major reports merit separate consideration because they usually involve coordinating team effort, although many of the techniques involved in writing them effectively are the same.

SHORT REPORTS

Having to read a report of just five pages can be an irritation to busy executives. Even when they do take the time to read it, there is a good chance that they won't read to the end if it isn't easy to follow. To write an effective report, whether it is giving information or recommending a course of action, you must:

- prepare it to interest your readers
- write it to have impact and in a way which is easy to follow
- make it look appealing on paper.

Interesting your readers

The ideas you choose to put in a report will naturally depend on its purpose. But, like speeches, they should also be ideas which will appeal to your audience. The techniques discussed in Chapter 2 will help you **analyse your readership**, giving you information such as:

- their level of education
- whether English is their first language
- their profession
- their level of authority
- their knowledge of the subject
- their interest in the subject
- their professional and personal needs
- the character of their organization, eg conservative or go-ahead.

Because reports are often specialized and may contain detailed information, there is a further step involved in deciding what will interest your readers.

ACTIVITY

Imagine you are preparing a report for a client, recommending the computerization of their order-processing system. What type of information will the following people in the client organization want from your report, and who will be the first person in the chain of approval for your recommendations?

managing director   *sales director*

personnel director   *data-processing manager*

first in the chain of approval:

GUIDELINES

Briefly, the type of information these readers would need might include:

managing director	*sales director*
long-term cost savings; short-term expense; ease of producing additional management information	disruption of work during changeover; ease of operation; implications for salesmen, eg paperwork

personnel director	*data-processing manager*
implications for staffing numbers, staff training and staff relations.	capabilities of the system; implementation time; costs.

The first person in the **chain of approval** for your recommendations is likely to be the data-processing manager. It will be his job to evaluate what you say and 'sell' the idea – or not – to his colleagues.

It is important to analyse your readership in this way because it determines the type of information you will include, the amount of technical language you can use, and how you will structure the report.

The main body of a report should be written for the readers who will first use the information, eg who have the power to take action on your recommendations. Information required by other readers should be given as an abstract, covering essential points of the report, or in appendices.

In the example used, the managing director would not be directly interested in details of the system, only what it could do, how much it would cost, etc, and would want to read an abstract. The data-processing manager might not want to know the full technical details of the system, but might want them verified by a specialist. These should be provided in an appendix.

The next step is to collect all the relevant information and express it in a way which your readers will find easy to follow and understand.

Writing your report

Reports, particularly those on technical subjects, will often be written to specifications given by a client or other people. So as well as collecting facts and figures, it is also important that all the relevant files and correspondence are read, including statements to be commented on, or questions to be answered.

The steps in writing a report then follow the same basic guidelines as those given in Chapter 3 for writing a speech, with a few changes.

Reports are **written for the eye**, unlike speeches which are written for the ear. This means that the audience can absorb information at their own pace. So the guidelines for keeping your message simple in a speech – limiting it to four main points – can be relaxed a little when you are writing a report. The only exceptions to this are when the subject is new to the intended readership, or its structure is unusual.

The **structure** you choose for a report will depend on its subject and its purpose, but it should encourage people to read, understand and accept your message.

ACTIVITY

What types of order can you use to present information which will help readers understand your report?

GUIDELINES

Even short reports are time-consuming to read. You can make it easier for the reader by dividing the information into sections which follow a logical sequence, eg problem, causes, possible solutions, best solution. Ways of putting ideas in a logical, easy to follow order, are discussed in Chapter 3.

In deciding what **writing style** to use, you may have to conform to house-style or professional conventions (eg in the legal and scientific worlds), but your first consideration must be your readers. It should be easy to read and understand.

ACTIVITY

This is a paragraph from a report whose main readership included non-specialists. List its good and bad points.

'Samples were taken from 50 comparable situations and showed a Poisson distribution which suggests that your problem is to be expected at this level of turnover. But we believe it can be easily overcome. It is recommended that you go ahead with your reorganization as soon as possible after the preliminary plans have been completed, and a simulation on the DTEC system has shown it to be a viable basis on which to operate.'

good and bad points

GUIDELINES   Good points are hard to find, but there are plenty of bad ones, eg:

- the sentences are too long and complex. 'Wordy' statements put readers off. Even if it's their job to read the report, they will be less interested in the task and less receptive to your message. Keep sentences short (about 20 words) and simple – they're easier to follow and have more impact

- paragraphs should also be short (three or four sentences). They're easier to follow and look less formidable

- unfamiliar words, jargon and acronyms (eg Poisson distribution, DTEC) should be avoided. Use words the reader knows well. They convey clear and precise information

- the phrase, 'It is recommended ...', sounds remote and lacks conviction – as if you are not willing to admit these are your recommendations. Using '*We* (or *I*) recommend ...' is more direct and convincing

- the use of verbs can have a similar effect, eg using 'We took samples from ...', instead of 'Samples were taken from...', gives a greater sense of your involvement in the report and its recommendations

- breaking the rules of grammar (eg '*But* we believe this can be *easily* overcome.') may be a deliberate choice to create greater impact or give it a more 'colloquial' tone. Consider your own reaction as a reader.

Although the rule for limiting yourself to four main points in a speech can be relaxed in a report, you should still aim to **keep your message as short and simple as possible.** There are three ways of reducing the length of a report without omitting essential information:

- state your ideas clearly; this helps to economize on words
- eliminate unnecessary words (eg 'we were *greatly* impressed')
- in the main body of the report only include information relevant to your main readership.

You can also make a report easier to read by the way you link ideas or sections. A brief introduction to each section giving a taste of what's to come, or summaries at the end of sections, will help readers follow and understand your message.

Making it look appealing

When you give a speech you can use your body as a visual aid to help get your ideas across effectively. In a report the layout of words on a page and the overall appearance play an equally important role. You can use layout and presentation to:

- make a report look more appealing to read
- make the task of reading less tiresome
- help you clarify information
- emphasize important points.

How can you achieve these things with the layout and general appearance of a report?

GUIDELINES Apart from illustrations, such as photographs, diagrams and graphs, you can use a range of 'visual' techniques to encourage people to read, understand and accept your message, eg:

- changes of typeface
- short paragraphs with wide margins and uniform spacing
- underlining
- listing points instead of writing one long paragraph
- numbering sections
- using good paper, an uncluttered and attractive cover, and a strong binding which opens flat.

First impressions are important: the first things that readers will see are the covering letter (discussed later), the cover and – if they thumb through the report – the layout of a page. Make these work for you, not against you.

MAJOR REPORTS

Writing major reports requires a slightly different approach. They are often collaborative projects, perhaps involving several colleagues, or other professionals in the same or different fields of work. The costs can be high, in man-hours as well as lost business, if they don't achieve results. Writing a major report efficiently involves:

- coordinating team effort
- pooling ideas
- writing drafts and getting feedback
- making it look readable.

Coordinating team effort

If you had to write an 80-page document, planning a schedule for the task would be a sensible first step. When there are several contributors involved it is essential.

Imagine you have been asked to write a report which must include contributions from several departments of your organization. Briefly describe how you would ensure that an effective report is delivered on time.

GUIDELINES

Unless you have the time and are qualified to supervise the contributions from each specialist department, you need to delegate responsibility. As the project leader you should select a team, of perhaps one senior person from each department, to help you coordinate the work. Together, this 'control' team can:

- decide what work is required and by whom
- agree a schedule of deadlines for receiving contributions, drafting the report, getting feedback, rewriting and delivery
- inform contributors of these arrangements
- monitor their progress to ensure that an effective report is delivered on time.

Never be too optimistic in setting deadlines. Allow time for unforeseen problems, even when the project seems straightforward. Delays irritate clients and hastily written reports don't achieve good results.

Pooling ideas

The preparation for writing a major report is basically the same as for a short report. The information must be gathered with the readers in mind.

ACTIVITY

What problems might there be in using material from many different contributors to write a report, and how could you overcome them?

GUIDELINES

In any team effort there will always be differences of opinion, however slight, and you can't afford to let these be seen in a report. It must show a common purpose and style of thinking. This is achieved by involving all members of the control team in:

- **idea production**, using a 'brainstorming' session (a group version of the technique outlined in Chapter 3), where ideas are listed quickly, without criticism or justification
- **writing objectives**, stating the purpose of the report and its parts
- **deciding an appropriate structure** for the report, its chapters and their sections, together with the *type* of support material that will be used.

The amount of information in major reports makes the choice of an effective structure very important. Dividing it into chapters, each with clearly marked sections and subsections, will make it easier for people to read and follow. The precise structure will depend on the purpose of the report, eg you may or may not be making recommendations.

ACTIVITY

What function is served by the following parts of a report?

an abstract

the introduction

appendices

GUIDELINES

These serve vital functions in a major report:

- **an abstract** is for the people who don't have time to read the report. It should cover the essentials, eg purpose of the report, findings, and recommendations, if any
- **the introduction** should grab the readers' attention, explain the purpose of the report and how it is presented
- **appendices** help keep the main body of the report uncluttered with diagrams, figures and other supporting information.

When the objectives and basic structure of the report have been agreed, members of the team take this information back to their own departments. The process can be repeated within each department to plan its own contribution to the report.

Using this technique ensures that all contributions are prepared with a common aim and structure, making the writer's task much easier.

Drafting and feedback

When you have received all the contributions, the writing process is the same as for a short report, with one major difference. The amount of information involved, some of which may be of a specialist nature and unfamiliar to you, makes it essential to get **feedback**.

Writing two, three, or even four drafts will enable you to incorporate criticism from the 'control' team and, if it's not yourself, the person with overall responsibility for the report.

You can use **the first draft** to get the basic structure on paper. Don't worry about including every detail, or your choice of words at this stage. When the group evaluates what you have written, check that all the relevant sections have been included, their order is correct, and that they will allow you to incorporate all the essential information.

When you write **subsequent drafts**, concentrate first on the content, then the writing style, and finally the layout and presentation.

Making it look readable

It is difficult to make an inch-thick report look appealing to read, but you can give the readers some encouragement.

The first thing they'll notice is the sheer bulk. Even if the subject is urgent, this can make them delay reading the report as long as possible. You can help overcome this feeling by showing clearly which parts are essential reading and which parts contain supporting documentation. Using coloured papers or dividers are common methods.

Once readers have opened the report, you should make it easy going for them by following the guidelines about page layout and general appearance described for short reports.

Letters

Despite predictions for the paperless office, letters are still the main method of communication between business organizations. Their sheer number can make them the most influential type of presentation made by an individual or organization. This section will help you learn how to write letters which:

- get read
- achieve their objectives
- help build a reputation for efficiency and clear thinking.

Letters often arrive in large numbers, unannounced, sometimes at busy periods, perhaps during a major crisis. The competition for the reader's time and attention can be enormous.

ACTIVITY

Imagine you have picked up a letter from your morning post. List the order in which you would normally scan its contents.

GUIDELINES

This activity gives you an idea of how people might react when they pick up one of your letters. First impressions are crucial. The following sequence of events is common:

1. You look for a name, address or logo on the envelope or, if it is already opened, the letterheading and author's name. When the sender is known to you, the letter will have created an instant impression and you will have certain expectations – either good or bad, depending on the impression they have created previously.

2. You look for a title. If it has one, your expectations are immediately focused on a particular subject. This is particularly important when the sender is unknown to you.

3. You read the opening sentence of the letter. At this point you might put the letter aside to deal with later.

4. You read the contents of the letter, and may put it aside at any time before you reach the end.

Because it is such a commonplace activity, too many people write letters without considering the impact they can achieve when carefully written. You can use the information above to ensure that when you write a letter it is well-received and stands a good chance of being given priority.

Preparation

Even the most straightforward letters require preparation – analysing your readers so that you can write your message in a way which appeals to them.

The **idea production** stage involves reading previous correspondence and relevant files, even if they are familiar to you, to ensure that you are providing all the information required (eg answers to questions). Information should then be checked to make sure it is relevant and accurate.

The next step is to organize this information into a clear and simple structure.

ACTIVITY

What are the different parts of a business letter and what purpose do they serve?

GUIDELINES

In addition to names, addresses and any reference to previous correspondence, business letters should have:

- a **short title** – three or four words at most – to focus attention on the subject of the letter
- a crisp **opening sentence** which takes advantage of the reader's initial phase of high interest to get the basic message across
- if the letter is long, it should have
  - an **introduction**, to whet the appetite and explain the structure of the letter,
  - **subheadings**, to help break up the information and revive the reader's interest, and
  - a **summary** of main points at the end
- a **concluding paragraph**, which takes advantage of the final burst of interest to tell the reader what happens next.

You may also need to enclose documents or other material with the letter. The significance of this material should always be mentioned in the body of the letter.

Writing style

All letters should be kept as clear and simple as possible. Some situations may require a **formal style**, notably in disciplines like the law, and where you know the reader favours the traditional formal approach. Otherwise a **conversational style** should be used, as if you were talking face-to-face with the reader. It is more direct and easier to understand.

The **overall tone** of the letter depends on the situation. You can make it sound 'chummy', or reflect your authority to write on the subject, by your choice of words. For example, starting a paragraph with, 'I don't believe there are any grounds for you to worry', can sound authoritative if your position and the contents of the letter back up your statement. Otherwise it may come across as careless or foolhardy.

The way you **end a letter** depends on the situation and your relationship with the reader. If the next move must come from them, throw the ball into their court. If not, explain what you will do next. Either way, make sure they know that you are eager to continue the relationship. If you know the reader well, you can end on a friendly or familiar note.

Letters can be taken as binding contracts, so don't make promises you can't keep. If you are writing about someone else, or another organization, be careful that what you say isn't libellous.

Layout and presentation

If they don't know you or your organization, readers will judge you by the way your letter looks as well as by what you say. This is usually an unconscious judgement, but it can have a powerful influence. To create a positive impression your letters should be:

- typed on good stationery
- divided into short paragraphs
- uniformly spaced
- centred on the page, with consistent margins
- error free.

Don't use letters simply to communicate specific information. Whether you write dozens of business letters each day, or just one occasionally, use them to create the type of professional image you want.

KEY POINTS

- first impressions are crucial – make it look appealing and easy to read
- write for the person who will take action
- keep it as short and simple as possible

SIGNPOST As soon as possible after writing your report or an important letter, assess how effectively you completed the task by reading Chapter 10.

8 SPEAKING UP FOR YOURSELF

Every time there is an audience you have the opportunity to create a positive impression, even when you are not making a formal presentation. This chapter is about three such occasions. It will help you to:

- build a reputation for clear thinking and efficiency through **meetings**
- create a positive image for yourself and your organization at **conferences**
- present the best possible 'you' at **interviews.**

Meetings

Many people view meetings as an interruption to their work, to be endured and conducted as quickly and with as little effort as possible. It is true that not all meetings are as efficient as they could be, and this does lead to time-wasting. But your conduct at meetings can enhance or damage your reputation.

For example, imagine the different impression each of these managers created on their colleagues even before they spoke:

A. sat back in the chair, legs outstretched, arms folded, staring into space

B. sat upright, turned to face the centre of the group, hands on the table, alert and maintaining eye-contact with every person attending.

Whether you plan to comment on an issue being discussed, or contribute spontaneously during the course of a meeting, you can use the occasion to enhance your reputation by:

- preparing to take an active role
- making your presence felt
- contributing effectively.

Preparing to take an active role

Preparation for a meeting should equip you to comment or to answer questions if the occasion arises.

Describe four of the steps in your preparation.

1.

2.

3.

4.

GUIDELINES

Preparation for a meeting doesn't end when the meeting starts. It ends when the meeting ends. To prepare effectively you should:

- study the agenda if there is one
  - does any topic relate directly to you or your area of operation?
  - is there a point on which you want to speak?
  - could discussion of anything else on the agenda implicate you?
- find out who is attending
  - could they raise subjects on which you need to respond? (see Chapter 2)
- prepare comments on issues you want to discuss and notes relating to questions you might be asked. Keep it short, simple and to the point. If it's more than a few sentences, give it an introduction and a conclusion (see Chapter 3)
- if you want to speak on a controversial issue, sound out others who will be attending for their views and support
- review your current work so that your knowledge is up-to-date
- listen carefully to everything that is said during the meeting
- make notes on the major points covered, particularly those which are relevant to you, and those on which you feel you can make useful comment.

Making your presence felt

Even when you are not speaking, you can use posture, gestures, facial expressions and eye-contact to show your active interest in the proceedings.

ACTIVITY

Write down how the following contribute to your appearance of being actively interested in what is going on in a meeting.

posture

gestures

facial expression

eye-contact

GUIDELINES

The influence of posture, gestures and eye-contact on an audience was discussed in Chapter 5. Using these effectively in a meeting follows a similar pattern, with some additional guidelines, eg:

- **posture:** upright, but relaxed, shows you are attentive. Leaning forward slightly as someone speaks shows your interest in their ideas. Your hands should be visible so that you can use them to gesture. Sitting close to the table and facing the centre of the group makes it easier to make eye-contact with everyone present
- **gestures:** nods of approval or agreement, hand movements, a shrug of the shoulders, and so on, show that you are alert to what is being said
- **facial expressions:** smiling, a quizzical look, frowning – your face reflects your subtlest feelings and shows that you're thinking about the ideas being exchanged
- **eye-contact:** maintaining eye-contact with all members of the meeting shows that you are interested in them as individuals and in their views.

Contributing effectively

Contributions to meetings, other than a formal presentation, fall into three categories:

- comments you have prepared beforehand
- answering questions
- spontaneous comments on issues raised (including asking questions).

ACTIVITY

Imagine you have prepared thoroughly and are asked a question during a meeting. In general terms, how would you answer, and what would you avoid?

GUIDELINES

The reasons people ask questions and guidelines on how to answer them effectively were discussed in Chapter 6. In general, for a meeting:

do	*don't*
if it's a formal meeting you may be required to stand up; it it's a very large meeting, stand anyway	show surprise or nervousness
be certain of the question – paraphrase it to make sure	direct your answer only to the questioner – address everyone present
focus on what you want to say; quickly decide your main points, your conclusion, and specific supporting ideas	ramble on – keep it short, simple and to the point
start talking as soon as possible – clearly and deliberately.	apologize if you don't have all the information with you – you can give it later.

Whether you are answering a question or just making a comment, **avoid destructive criticism.** It can earn you a reputation for narrow thinking. Try to phrase your comments in a positive way. Acknowledge the positive side of other speakers' comments first, and *then* the drawbacks.

Other ways of contributing to meetings include helping to keep the proceedings on course and encouraging contributions from other people present. You can ask to go back to previous items, to move on to vital issues, ask for the views of specific individuals, and so on. If it's a formal meeting, this is often done through the chairman.

Remember: the way you contribute to a meeting affects your reputation as well as decisions that are made.

Conferences

Conferences are used more and more to communicate ideas within and between professions. Most people attend simply to listen to those ideas, ignoring the opportunity to use it as a platform to introduce themselves and their organization. This can be done simply and effectively by asking questions of the speakers, or speaking during discussion periods.

Any contribution you make at a conference must create a positive image among the speakers and the audience, which may include specialists in your own and other disciplines. This involves learning how to prepare and deliver your question or contribution with appropriate impact.

Preparation

The preparation for speaking 'off-the-cuff' at a conference is similar to that for a meeting, and ends when the conference ends, not when it starts. But because the audience is less likely to know you and your organization, your contributions should create an image for them.

What preparation can you do *before* a conference?

GUIDELINES

When you arrive at a conference you should already have a good idea of the subjects on which you may want to comment. To prepare effectively you should:

- make a note of which subjects to be presented are related to your area of operation and those which interest you
- make checklists of what you would like to know about each one
- write brief comments about your own experience and that of your organization, relevant to the main aspects of each subject.

Take these notes with you to the conference and then, during the conference:

- mark the points covered in each presentation (and during question or discussion periods) on your checklists
- if something is omitted which interests you, write a question to ask the speaker
- during each presentation make notes on topics of interest, particularly those of which you and your organization have experience.

Your notes should form the basis of anything you say at the conference. Don't introduce irrelevant points. It will create the impression that either you haven't been listening, or you are saying it for your own benefit.

Making your contribution

Conference notes will often indicate discussion or question periods, and some speakers will confirm, at the beginning of their presentation, that they are happy to answer questions at the appropriate time.

You should have time to write your question or contribution during the relevant presentation.

ACTIVITY

How can you highlight yourself or your organization in what you say?

GUIDELINES You should start by clearly stating *your name and your organization*. What you say next depends on the situation but, if possible, include information from one of the comments you prepared about your experience of the subject being discussed. This will give continued prominence to you and your organization, and may even lead to you being asked questions about your experience.

The general guidelines for speaking at a conference are similar to those for meetings:

- use your voice and body to draw attention to your words
- speak to the whole audience
- speak clearly, keeping comments simple and to the point
- make questions positive and straightforward. Don't criticize or try to catch the speaker out – it creates a bad impression
- if lengthy comments are absolutely necessary, give them an introduction, middle and conclusion (see Chapter 3).

In the hot seat – being interviewed

Even the most practised interviewee can feel nervous at the prospect of being put in the hot seat if the outcome is important. Whatever the purpose of the interview (eg job selection, or appraisal of your current job), the uncertainty of the situation can get in the way of presenting yourself effectively. You can increase your chances of success by:

- preparing to answer and ask questions intelligently and effectively
- projecting a positive image.

Preparation

The purpose of preparing for an interview is to minimize the uncertainties of the situation. Both you and the interviewer will want information from each other. You can make quite accurate predictions of the type of questions you will be asked, and decide what you want to know.

ACTIVITY   Write down what information you and the interviewer might want to find out through a job interview.

the interviewer	*you*

GUIDELINES In general terms this is the type of information you will both expect to exchange:

the interviewer	*you*
why are you applying?	what are the main duties of the job?
what relevant experience do you have?	what are the qualities and qualifications required?
what can you contribute?	to whom would you be responsible?
do you know what the job involves?	what are the working conditions?
what previous jobs have you most enjoyed and why?	what are the problems in the job?
what career plans do you have?	what is the salary and other benefits?
what outside interests do you have?	what facilities are there (work and recreation)?
	is training offered?
	what are the prospects?

If it is a job in a specialist field, you may be asked questions designed to test your knowledge and find out your professional interests and feeling for the job. You may be asked about recent developments in your professional field – what you know about them and your opinion of their importance.

Prepare concise answers to all the questions you might be asked and consider whether they will create the impression that you are the best candidate for the job. Be positive. Concentrate on your skills and achievements. Don't lie – just present the truth in a way that will create the best possible impression. Whatever you can find out about the organization before the interview will help you create the impression of interest in working for them.

You can repeat this process for other types of interview. For example, in an interview to appraise your current job, you might be asked such questions as:

- what do you enjoy most and least about the job?
- what have you achieved?
- are you dissatisfied with any aspects of the job?
- how could it be improved?
- how could you improve?
- would you need help, and of what type?

Projecting a positive image

There are basically three things that you can control to influence the interviewer:

- first impressions
- what you say
- how you say it.

The **first seconds** of an interview are a critical period. Walk with a steady, measured pace; upright, but relaxed; smile, and keep your right hand free to shake. Your greeting should be polite but not gushing.

Your dress and general appearance is obviously important. Try to conform to what you think is expected, looking clean, tidy and comfortable. Don't overdress – it can create the impression of poor judgement, or of trying to compensate for lack of confidence.

When you sit, make yourself comfortable and try to look relaxed. There will usually be a brief period of ice-breaking, when the interviewer makes a comment such as:

'You managed to find us OK, then?' or
'I see you've got a copy of our annual report.'

Use the opportunity to start contributing, eg:

'Yes, I've passed here before on my way to ...'
'Yes, I was interested to see the diversity of
the company's operations.'

Don't answer just 'yes' or 'no'. That will force the interviewer to look for another way of opening the conversation. From the start, you should appear eager to contribute.

Having prepared thoroughly, you should know what to say in response to most of the interviewer's questions. Remember to concentrate on your skills and achievements; support your answers with details of your experience and, if you are asked to give an opinion, include the reasons why you feel as you do.

ACTIVITY   What impression might be created by the following ways of answering a question?

way of answering	impression created
pausing briefly before answering	
hesitant, nervously stumbling over the words	
clearly and confidently	
quickly and loudly	
briefly and simply	

GUIDELINES

How you answer a question will make a powerful impression on the interviewer, eg:

way of answering	impression created
pausing briefly before answering	thoughtful
hesitant, nervously stumbling over the words	unsure of yourself or the subject
clearly and confidently	believable
quickly and loudly	over-confident, immature or nervous
briefly and simply	clear-thinking

Listen carefully when you are asked a question. Pause briefly before you answer to collect your thoughts. Speak clearly, deliberately and with meaning (see Chapter 5). Keep your answers short, simple and to the point.

Finally, your **body language** – posture, gestures, facial expression and eye-contact – should reflect a natural and honest image. Use it to show your involvement and interest in the interview. Watch for responses from the interviewer. Does he believe what you're saying? Is he interested in this particular aspect of your experience? Adapt to his response. If you sense that he wants to speak, ask one of the questions you have prepared. That way you can get him to do more of the talking.

KEY POINTS

- be prepared for likely questions and topics you want to discuss
- establish your presence with your posture, gestures, facial expressions and eye-contact
- speak clearly and confidently
- make your contributions relevant, clear and to the point.

SIGNPOST

While it's still fresh in your mind, assess how effective you were by reading Chapter 10.

9 REACHING THE MASSES

The media are becoming more and more accessible. In television, radio and the press, there is a growing demand for people with views and ideas to express.

When the opportunity to reach a mass audience through the media comes your way, you stand little chance of getting your message across effectively unless you understand how they work and are well-prepared. At worst, with a few ill-chosen words, you can destroy your reputation, your colleagues', and that of your organization within seconds.

This chapter will help you use the media to your advantage by learning:

- **how to prepare** for a media interview
- **specific techniques** to ensure that you always get your message across.

Preparing for a media interview

There are two important differences between reaching an audience through the media and through other types of presentation. Firstly, editorial guidelines and programme formats dictate what type of information is used by the media and how it is presented.

Secondly, instead of addressing your audience directly, you will nearly always have an intermediary – the interviewer. They are trained professionals – trained to sniff out a story, trained to ask searching questions, trained to interpret answers, and trained to make themselves look good.

If you want to get your message across effectively you must know:

- what the media want
- what type of questions to expect
- how your answers will be interpreted
- how to get your message across in your answers.

What do the media want?

To get your message across effectively in any presentation, you must target it to appeal to the needs and interests of your audience. With the media there's no direct way of finding out this information, but fortunately they've done it for you. The media spend millions of pounds each year analysing their audiences. Provide what the media want and you will reach an audience they have already targeted.

ACTIVITY

Imagine you have just been asked by the press to give an interview. What questions would you feel it wise to ask them?

GUIDELINES

If you are to make good use of this opportunity you will need to prepare, so you will want to know as much as possible. They'll offer some of this information without you asking, but you need to know:

- which newspaper or magazine?
- why are you asking me?
- is it for a news or feature item?
- what's the subject?
- what's the 'angle' (the central theme)?
- when will it appear (coinciding with a particular event)?
- how long will it be (brief or in-depth)?
- who else is being interviewed (rivals or supporters)?
- how much time will it take (how much time will you have to get your message across)?
- who will be doing the interview? (so that you can find out the style of their work, eg sympathetic, thrusting, analytical)
- what type of questions will I be asked?

You need the same type of information if you are approached by radio or television. It will give you an idea of how questions will be phrased, the general mood of the interview, and what is expected of you. If you don't find out, the consequences can be disastrous.

> A prominent businessman was invited to appear on a television programme to discuss the implications of recent changes in government financial policies. He was well-versed in the subject and, with a bit of preparation, he went along to the studio armed with answers to all the questions he thought they could ask.
>
> It wasn't until he walked on to the studio set that it dawned on him what the programme involved: he sat alone, on a pedestal, facing a panel of union officials.
>
> The answers he had prepared were useless. In a few words the union representatives conjured up images of countless government injustices against unions. The businessman didn't stand a chance of giving his expert opinion on the real significance of the new policies. All that came across to the audience was a picture of the downtrodden unions.

By asking a few more questions before appearing, the businessman could have avoided an embarrassing situation which did nothing to help his reputation.

What questions will I be asked?

Although you will often be told in advance what type of questions to expect, it is wise to prepare your own list of likely questions, because:

- you may *not* be told questions in advance, eg if your views are newsworthy a reporter may unexpectedly telephone you at home or in the office, or stop you in the street for comment
- you may have little time to prepare your answers after being told the questions
- the interviewer may slip in an extra question, perhaps prompted by the way you have answered an earlier one
- preparing answers to likely questions helps get your message clear in your mind.

To predict what questions you are likely to be asked you need to know what information the media want from you. Even when they tell you, often it will be in very general terms and there is no law which prevents them from raising other subjects. The following technique will help you compile a list of questions they could ask:

- make a list of your answers to the questions, 'What am I doing or involved with that could interest them?' and, 'What ideas or views do I have that they want to hear?', remembering that they may be personal as well as professional
- then write down what aspects of each one the media could ask you about – the pros and cons, the good and bad news, the good and bad image.

If you prepare thoroughly in this way you won't be caught off-guard by an interviewer.

ACTIVITY

Imagine you are an investigative journalist and have been given a tip about possible corruption in 'high places'. Write down four general questions you will be asking yourself as you pursue the story.

1.

2.

3.

4.

GUIDELINES   The media want 'interesting' news – which often means controversy, deception, crisis, injustice, and so on. In situations like this they would be asking themselves questions such as:

- who's involved?
- are there far-reaching consequences?
- is this the tip of the iceberg?
- there's the smoke, where's the fire?
- is something being concealed?
- are there political overtones?

Interviewers may ask you probing questions and you must be prepared to answer them convincingly.

Even under normal circumstances, the media often want contributions at short notice, but dealing with media interest during crises and similar events is especially difficult. Many organizations have 'crisis management' plans which provide guidelines for dealing with these situations. If you want to take full advantage of media interest when it occurs, you should also be prepared.

How will your message be interpreted?

In the media, like any other type of spoken presentation, you are judged as much by how you say something as what you say. Interviewers learn to read non-verbal signals, using them to interpret your message and direct the questioning. In a radio or television interview the audience can also pick up these signals as part of your message. For example:

- losing your temper with an interviewer may suggest that the last question touched a raw nerve – the embarrassing truth
- fiddling nervously with a pen, clasping your hands tightly together, or speaking with an uneven voice, can be taken to mean that you are unsure of yourself or of the facts, or are not telling the truth
- raising your voice may sound as if you are trying to win by force, because your argument is weak.

Your voice, posture, gestures, expression and eye-contact with the interviewer should reinforce what you are saying (this subject is discussed again later). If your body and tone of voice say one thing, and your words another, the interviewer, and perhaps your audience, will sense the inconsistency.

Preparing your message

Although the basic guidelines for organizing your ideas into an effective message are the same as those outlined in Chapter 3, there are some additional problems to be overcome, eg:

- the time or space you are given may be limited
- you may be competing with a major news story which has broken the same day
- your audience may be distracted, eg the basic necessities of life, like eating, interrupt television viewing
- your audience may range from people with little or no schooling, to the most distinguished intellectuals.

ACTIVITY

Bearing these factors in mind, what should be the main features of an effective message for getting across in the media?

GUIDELINES

To have the best chance of reaching a large audience and having the desired effect, your message should be:

- **short**: particularly for radio and television, where you may have a maximum of two or three minutes to get your points across. The briefer the points, the greater the chance that your audience will listen. Use three main points at most and put them in order of importance – you may only have time to get one across. Even in press interviews, where you may have more time, they like short quotes encapsulating your main points
- **simple**: use plain English and simple sentences. They have more impact and are easier to understand. If you speak down to any sector of your audience they may become angry and oppose your ideas, or simply ignore you. Even press reporters sometimes have to spend time interpreting interviews and then your message loses impact. If you have to use technical terms, explain them
- **interesting**: use anecdotes and analogies which relate to everyday life, particularly for radio and television – it makes your points relevant to the widest possible audience and holds their attention.

Even if you are going to talk for one minute on your local radio station, or chat over lunch with a 'friendly' reporter, don't rely on your knowledge or natural skill with words. Preparation crystallizes your thoughts on a subject, sharpens your thinking and will help you answer difficult questions convincingly.

Don't overstate your case. It is a great temptation when you have only minutes to get your message across, but it may not sound credible. Simply give the good news and be prepared when the interviewer probes for the bad news.

If you are speaking on behalf of someone else, or an organization, get their agreement on what you intend to say, particularly if it's a controversial issue. Otherwise you may find yourself out on a limb if they later disclaim what you've said.

Techniques for winning with the media

Although the three branches of the media have many things in common, there are major differences that affect the way you should deliver your message. They all reach a mass audience and are therefore a very influential platform for expressing ideas, but to use them effectively you must understand their particular methods of working.

One thing you should do **before meeting the media** – whether it's the press, radio or television – is to learn your main points until you can express them in many different ways. Although the interviewer may discuss many aspects of the subject, the more times you can state your main points, without repeating your words, the greater the chance of getting them across to your audience. It's better to repeat one point over and over, than cover several points once.

Keeping your comments to the point also prevents the discussion from straying, when the interviewer could raise matters you are not prepared to discuss.

SPEAKING TO THE PRESS

The press provides the greatest opportunity of all the media for you to reach a large audience. From the national daily newspapers to specialist journals published once a year, it covers every conceivable subject and interest. Ideas can be explored in detail and there is a permanent record of your views which may still be read months or even years later.

The main problem with the press is that you have less control over your message than with radio or television. Many journalists now use tape recorders for interviews, which guards against you being inadvertently misquoted. But you have little way of knowing how they will *interpret* what you have said when they write the story.

This is what one town planner said during an interview about a proposed major new relief road:

'It's going to reduce heavy traffic in the centre of the town remarkably. Local shopkeepers have been complaining for years that it's damaging their trade, and of course local residents are delighted at the prospect of peace and quiet at last. It will involve demolishing about 25 houses along the route, and naturally those residents are angry. But in comparison with the benefits for the town, their inconvenience is a minor consideration.'

This is how the journalist interpreted his answer:

'Ernest Hapless, town planner for Wellford, doesn't foresee any problems in getting the go-ahead for the major new relief road. He said the fact that about 25 families would lose their homes was "a minor consideration".'

Although not all journalists would take the same line, you have to guard against being misinterpreted, whether intentionally or not.

ACTIVITY

Write a list of guidelines for dealing with the press effectively, which would avoid this and similar problems.

If you stick to some simple rules, you can get the press coverage you want and still provide a good story for the journalist, eg:

- don't take reporters into your confidence, however friendly they seem. Even if you state that, 'This is off the record', they can reflect what you've said in the tone of the story they write
- don't expect them to have the same view of the situation. Unless you state your case precisely, they can interpret what you say to reflect their own views
- don't say more than you intended to say. Keep to your three points, otherwise the reporter may use insignificant things you've said and your message will be distorted
- don't let them put words in your mouth – answer questions fully; if you deny only part of a question the reporter may take it that you accept the other part
- never say, 'No comment'. Even if your reasons are honest and straightforward, it can be misinterpreted, eg: 'He refused to comment when asked to confirm reports of corruption'.

The press can be your best friend or your worst enemy. Developing a good working relationship with them is in your own interests. So be honest, straightforward and, whenever possible, supply the information they ask for.

TALKING ON THE RADIO

After the press, radio is the next most accessible medium for reaching a large audience. It provides national and regional news coverage, as it happens, 24 hours a day, and there are regular feature programmes where people air their views on a wide range of subjects.

People listen to the radio more than they do to television because it doesn't demand all their attention – they can listen while they're doing something else. So radio works hard at interesting listeners with the content of its programmes, and this can be to your advantage. But radio also has its drawbacks.

What are the major drawbacks and what ways are there to overcome them?

GUIDELINES

The most obvious problem with the radio is that you only have your voice to get your message across. You can't use gestures and facial expressions to get attention, help the audience understand, or give your words impact. So you have to be especially careful about what you say and how you say it.

Listeners are interested in things which relate to their own experience, so anecdotes and analogies can be powerful tools when you are speaking on the radio. They help your audience recognize the significance of what you are saying, eg:

> 'At one time the only thing that kept my wife and I awake was our baby son crying. Then, when cot deaths hit the headlines, it was Christopher not crying that kept us awake. Today, thanks to this new monitoring system, babies can sleep safely and their parents soundly.'

Another problem with radio is that you have to work harder at projecting your enthusiasm. Ways of doing this were discussed in Chapter 6. Remember that your voice can reflect boredom if you sound tired, and lack of conviction if you sound nervous. Practise speaking your main points with a lively voice which is crisp and clear.

To prevent people being distracted from listening by whatever else they're doing, the pace on radio tends to be fast to maintain interest. This has several consequences:

- you may have less than 30 seconds at a time to speak – so keep your points as brief as possible
- 'ums' and 'ahs' irritate listeners used to the fast pace – it makes you sound uncertain and unconvincing. Make sure you know what you want to say
- you don't have much time to think, so you may want to use notes. But remember to make your words sound spontaneous
- if you are on a panel competing with other speakers in a 'free-for-all', speak up the instant there's a gap.

If you are interrupted before you finish making a point, raise your voice slightly and continue. If the person persists, say something like, 'Can I just finish my point and then I'll answer your question'. *Don't* be sidetracked and leave your point incomplete.

It is especially important when talking on radio and television to correct the interviewer, or anyone else, if they make inaccurate comments. Don't leave it until later in the programme – you may not get time to correct them, and even if you do, by that time the audience will have accepted the inaccuracy.

Finally, if you get an unexpected telephone call from a radio station, establish immediately whether you are 'on air'. In the unlikely even that you are, you'll have to collect you thoughts quickly. If not, and they want to record your comments for use later, ask if you can phone them back. This will give you time to prepare.

APPEARING ON TELEVISION

Television is widely accepted as the most believable of the media. Viewers feel more confident in judging what they can see happening as well as hear. It is also the most 'intimate' medium and is the closest thing you can get to a one-to-one conversation with 20 million people simultaneously.

Because television demands all our attention, eyes as well as ears, there is a strong temptation to switch off or change channels at moments we find it uninteresting. To overcome this temptation, television has to use a more cut-and-thrust approach than radio. One aspect of this is that television journalists often try to trigger a strong response in people they are interviewing, eg:

- by asking unexpected questions
- looking for weaknesses in an argument
- phrasing questions in a provocative way.

Reactions to these tactics like surprise or anger, which are difficult to hide, will make you seem less credible. Thorough preparation is the best defence.

If you are interrupted before you finish making a point, or inaccurate information is quoted, use the techniques recommended for dealing with these situations on the radio.

General images stick in the mind better than specific ideas, and viewers' lasting impression of you and, by association, your message, will come from your general manner more than from what you say.

ACTIVITY

Describe in detail the features of your voice and manner that help to make you appear sincere and convincing. (If you get stuck, they were discussed in Chapter 5.)

GUIDELINES   Your posture, gestures and facial expressions are particularly important on television. Apart from close-ups, which can highlight the slightest nervous twitch, television tends to exaggerate all your responses. The way you speak is also important; it has to suit the 'intimate' nature of television. To appear sincere and convincing:

- speak as if you were in normal conversation with someone, but remembering to use the full range of your voice to make it sound clear and meaningful
- avoid long pauses, either when asked a question or between sentences. If they are expecting you to speak, viewers will think you can't answer
- if you need notes, make them unobtrusive. You'll appear more convincing and authoritative if you don't use them
- talk to the interviewer, not the camera, otherwise it will look unnatural
- sit upright and slightly forward in your chair; it makes you look and feel alert
- use gestures and facial expressions as you would in normal conversation. Don't exaggerate; let them come naturally from your enthusiasm
- avoid nervous habits like fiddling with a tie or pulling down the hem of a skirt; they can distract viewers from what you are saying
- dress to suit the occasion, and check tie, make-up, zips, hair, and so on. A careless appearance rubs off on your opinions.

Finally, television technology has certain limitations. The cameras are not as efficient as the human eye and tend to distort things, so be careful what you wear. Avoid narrow stripes, small checks, very loud or clashing colours, and anything that will catch the light (eg excessive jewellery and shiny materials). The way cameras react to these can be a total distraction for viewers.

This chapter should help give you the confidence to take any opportunity you are offered to express your views through the media. But if you are still unsure, remember that without you there to state your case, your competitors or rivals will have a free hand in speaking against you. If it's a crisis situation the facts will speak (perhaps unfairly) for themselves.

The media are very influential. If you get the opportunity to use them, take it, and do everything you can to make them work for you, not against you.

KEY POINTS

- whatever the media want, you have your own message to get across
- anticipate questions and learn what you want to say
- keep it short, simple and to the point
- don't let them put words in your mouth, and correct any inaccuracies
- make your voice and body count – work at being sincere and convincing.

SIGNPOST

If you have time *before* presenting your views in the media, you can rehearse using the guidelines given in Chapter 5.

As soon as possible *afterwards*, assess how you handled the situation by reading Chapter 10.

10 WHERE TO NEXT?

At the end of Chapters 6 to 9 I recommended that as soon as possible after making a presentation, while it's still fresh in your mind, you should assess your performance by reading this chapter.

The best way to improve your presentation skills is to get feedback about your performance, so that you can learn from your mistakes. The four questionnaires in this chapter will help you identify major areas where you can improve before you next:

- make a speech
- write a report or an important letter
- contribute to a meeting, conference or interview, or
- speak to the media.

ACTIVITY

Complete the questionnaire which is appropriate to the type of presentation you have made. If a question is irrelevant, leave it out.

Speeches

No | *Yes*

(tick yes or no)

Did you feel detached from the audience?

Did your nervousness get in the way of acting naturally?

Was there any information you feel you should have made clearer?

Do you think you sounded unconvincing at any time?

Could you have made your central theme clearer?

Could you have given your speech more impact?

Did you feel uncertain about what you wanted to say at any point?

Did you forget, at any time, to watch how individual members of your audience were reacting to what you said?

Or fail to respond to how they felt?

If you used aids, did they seem to interrupt the flow of your speech?

Were there any problems that you could have foreseen?

Did the end of your speech seem to fall flat?

Were you asked any questions that you thought you had answered in your speech?

Do you feel you could have done better with more practice?

Add up the number of ticks in the *yes* column and then read page 138.

Reports and letters

No | *Yes*

(tick yes or no)

Does the appearance of what you have produced reflect the type of image you want?

Have you included all the information you wanted to include?

And all the information you were asked for?

Did you make a conscious effort to restrict yourself to only that information which was necessary?

Does it convey the meaning you originally intended?

Is the information easy to follow?

Is there a consistent theme throughout?

Did you take special care over your introduction and conclusion?

Have you divided the information into sections so that it is easy to digest?

Have you used any words that your readers will find difficult to understand?

Are the sentences short, simple and direct?

Did you choose your writing style for your readers?

Did you meet the deadline you set yourself?

Did it turn out 100 per cent as you would have liked?

Add up the number of ticks in the *no* column and then read page 138.

Meetings, conferences and interviews

	No	Yes

(tick yes or no)

Did you look alert and eager to contribute?

Did you make a significant contribution?

Did you keep your comments short and simple?

When you spoke, did you sound confident in what you were saying?

Did you use gestures and facial expressions to support what you said?

Did you get the response you expected to everything you said?

Did you phrase your questions in a simple and straightforward way?

Did you get all the information you wanted from the situation?

Had you prepared for all the questions you were asked?

Was everything you said directly relevant to the situation?

As a result of what you said, do you think they knew everything you wanted them to know?

On reflection, were you well prepared?

Do you feel now that you covered *all* the important points?

Do you think the image you wanted to create came across effectively?

If you could do it again, would you do it exactly the same?

Add up the number of ticks in the *no* column and then read page 138.

The media

	No	*Yes*

(tick yes or no)

Was there anything you feel you should have known before giving the interview?

Do you think the interviewer had more control over the situation than you?

Did you give out signals in your voice, face or gestures which didn't match what you were saying?

Were you visibly nervous or unsure of yourself?

Did you say anything which didn't contribute directly to what you wanted to achieve?

Did you say anything that you now regret having said?

Was emphasis given to anything other than your main points?

Did you ramble on at any point?

Did you feel intimidated by any of the questions?

Did any of the questions leave you lost for words?

Could you have got your message across more effectively?

Could you have made your comments more interesting and relevant to the audience?

Could you have answered any of the questions more effectively given more time?

If you could do it again, would you change what you said or how you said it?

Add up the number of ticks in the *yes* column and then read page 138.

GUIDELINES It is impossible to cover any of these subjects in depth with so few questions, but your answers give an indication of how effectively you made your presentation. **The higher your score the more you need to improve your presentation skills.**

This book should have helped you recognize what is involved in making effective presentations, and to some extent have helped you overcome your weaknesses. But there are some aspects of making presentations, particularly to a live audience, which are difficult to learn from a book.

Whatever your score, there is always scope for improving your presentation skills and you would benefit from a traditional training course. These have several advantages:

- subjects can be covered in outline or in depth, depending on your needs and the time you can spare
- often courses can be tailor-made to meet your precise needs, including preparation and rehearsal for specific presentations you have to make
- you can get immediate expert feedback on your performance to help you improve.

After using this book you should be able to decide what type of training would help you most.

KEY POINTS
- recognize your weaknesses
- have confidence that you can overcome them with more training
- decide which way is best for you.

SIGNPOST The Directory which follows lists organizations offering specialist training in how to make effective presentation. You can use it to select the type of training which would benefit you most.

	talks and speeches	closed-circuit tv	visual aids	effective writing	the press	radio	television
Advanced Marketing Management Ltd 13–15 Church Street Welwyn Hertfordshire AL6 9LN Telephone: 043871 5011 Telex: 826542 Contact: Mr Larry Monk	•	•	•	•			
Jane Allan & Co Kingsbrook Monxton Hampshire SP11 8AW Telephone: 0264 710143 Contact: Jane Allan	•		•	•	•		
Beetik Limited 2 Woodland Rise Muswell Hill London N10 3UG Telephone: 01-883 5819 Contact: Stephen Allender	•		•	•	•		
Gordon Bell and Partners 505 Garratt Lane London SW18 4SW Telephone: 01-870 3641 Contact: Ms Geraldine Naqui	•		•	•	•		

	talks and speeches	closed-circuit tv	visual aids	effective writing	the press	radio	television
BIS Applied Systems Ltd 20 Upper Ground London SE1 9PN Telephone: 01-633 0866 Telex: 919642 Contact: Ms E M Priestley	•	•	•	•			
Blackwood Hodge Management Centre Nene College Park Campus Northampton NN2 7AL Telephone: 0604 719531 Contact: Sue Laste (Course co-ordinator)	•	•					
Blomfield Gunn Associates 7 Tabor Grove Wimbledon London SW19 4EB Telephone: 01-947 5045 Contact: John B Gunn	•		•	•			
British Association for Commercial and Industrial Education (BACIE) 16 Park Crescent London W1N 4AP Telephone: 01-636 5351 Telex: 268350 ICSA Contact: Janet Goddard	•	•	•	•			
British Institute of Management Management House Cottingham Road Corby Northants NN17 1TT Telephone: 0536 204222 Contact: Operations Centre	•	•	•	•	•	•	•
Building Advisory Service 18 Mansfield Street London W1M 9FG Telephone: 01-636 2862 Telex: 265763 Contact: Annette O'Sullivan	•	•		•			

	talks and speeches	closed-circuit tv	visual aids	effective writing	the press	radio	television
Burton Manor College Burton South Wirral Cheshire L64 5SJ Telephone: 051-336 5172 Contact: Paula Irvine	•	•	•	•		•	•
The Canning School 4 Abingdon Road London W8 6AF Telephone: 01-937 3233 Telex: 291467 CANNIN G Contact: John Stuart Milne	•	•	•	•	•	•	•
Cargill Attwood International 8 Teddington Park Teddington TW11 8DA Telephone: 01-977 8091 Telex: 23152 (Ref: 8360) Contact: Thomas J Attwood (Director)	•		•	•			
The Certified Accountants Educational Trust PO Box 244 29 Lincoln's Inn Fields London WC2A 3EE Telephone: 01-242 6855 x 848 Telex: 24381 CERTAC Contact: Miss Clare O'Sullivan	•	•	•	•			
Charnwood Management Centre Ltd Langley House Langley Mill Nottingham NG16 4AN Telephone: 0773 530777 Contact: Richard Johnson	•		•				
Clark Whitehill Consultants Ltd 25 New Street Square London EC4A 3LN Telephone: 01–353 1577 Telex: 887422 Contact: Chris Robinson	•	•	•	•			

	talks and speeches	closed-circuit tv	visual aids	effective writing	the press	radio	television
CMTC Management Training Centre Woodland Grange Leamington Spa Warwickshire CU32 6RN Telephone: 0926 36621 Contact: Mr S Johnston (Director) or H Mousley	●	●	●	●			
Communication Improvements Ltd Sentry House Frimley Road Camberley GU15 2QN Telephone: 0276 66446 Telex: 858386 Contact: Ian Harrison	●	●	●	●			
Crawley College of Technology College Road Crawley West Sussex RH10 1NR Telephone: 0293 512574 Contact: Mr G R Simpson	●	●	●	●			
C.T.V.C. Hillside Studios Merry Hill Road Bushey Herts WD2 1DR Telephone: 01-950 4426 Contact: Ann Weir-Rhodes (Training Co-ordinator)	●	●	●		●	●	●
Datasolve Education Glen House Stag Place London SW1E 5AG Telephone: 01-828 7878 Telex: 296660 Contact: Joan Clarke	●	●	●	●			

	talks and speeches	closed-circuit tv	visual aids	effective writing	the press	radio	television
Dunchurch Tutorial Learning Services Dunchurch Rugby Warwickshire CV22 6QW Telephone: 0788 810656 Telex: 0788 311879 Contact: Catherine Park (Customer Liaison)	•	•	•				
Educational Foundation for Visual Aids The George Building Normal College Bangor Gwynedd LL57 2PZ Telephone: 0248 370144 Contact: B Mullett	•	•	•			•	
Effective Speaking Ltd 61 High Street Stone Staffs ST15 8AD Telephone: 0785 813558 Contact: Tony Handy	•	•	•			•	•
EELA: Management Advisory & Training Services 23 Essex Street London WC2R 3AR Telephone: 01-240 2591 Fax: 01-836 8845 Contact: E Cater	•	•	•	•			
Equaville Ltd Elmsmead Princes Road Bourne End Bucks SL8 5HZ Telephone: 06285 25210 Contact: Terence Sharkey (Director)	•	•	•	•	•	•	•

	talks and speeches	closed-circuit tv	visual aids	effective writing	the press	radio	television
Fielden House Productivity Centre Ltd Mersey Road West Didsbury Manchester M20 8QA Telephone: 061-445 2426 Telex: 665305 FIELDN G Contact: J T Coulter	•	•	•	•			
Guardian Business Services Ltd 119 Farringdon Road London EC1R 3DA Telephone: 01–278 6787 Contact: The Registrar	•	•	•	•			
Guild Sound & Vision Ltd 6 Royce Road Peterborough PE1 5YB Telephone: 0733 315315 Telex: 32683 Contact: Training Division	•		•				
The Institute of Chartered Accountants of Scotland 27 Queen Street Edinburgh EH2 1LA Telephone: 031-225 5673 Contact: A W Young	•	•	•	•			
The Institute of Directors 116 Pall Mall London SW1Y 5ED Telephone: 01-839 1233 Contact: Derek Coltman	•	•	•				•
The Institute of Management Education 7 Westbourne Road Southport PR8 2HZ Telephone: 0704 67994 Contact: Derek J Wake (Principal)	•		•	•			

	talks and speeches	closed-circuit tv	visual aids	effective writing	the press	radio	television
The Institution of Industrial Managers Rochester House 66 Little Ealing Lane London W5 4XX Telephone: 01-579 9411 Contact: Mr S J Collop (Secretary for Education)	•			•			
Invicta Training Ltd 6 The Broadway London SE6 4SP Telephone: 01-690 9931 Contact: Michele Burke (Sales & Marketing Manager)	•			•			
Frank Jefkins School of Public Relations 84 Ballards Way South Croydon Surrey CR2 7LA Telephone: 0689 47282 Telex: 8952560 ASTEN G Contact: Mrs Angela Davies (Courses Secretary)				•			
Lea Storey & Co Ltd 14 Charlotte Street Bristol BS19 5PT Telephone: 0272 211964/5 Contact: Courses Secretary	•	•	•	•	•	•	•
Leadership Development Ltd 495 Fulham Road London SW6 1HH Telephone: 01-381 6233 Contact: Catherine Hibbert	•		•				
Lynch Greenland & Partners Ltd Highfield House The Warren Ashtead Surrey KT21 2SL Telephone: 03722 75094 Contact: Mrs Hazel Matthews	•		•	•			

	talks and speeches	closed-circuit tv	visual aids	effective writing	the press	radio	television
Marketing Improvements Ltd Ulster House 17 Ulster Terrace Outer Circle Regents Park London NW1 4PJ Telephone: 01-487 5811 Telex: 299723 MARIMP G Contact: Patrick Forsyth (Client Services Director)	•		•	•			
Marketing Technology Ltd 6 Calstone Calne Wiltshire SN11 8PY Telephone: 0249 817341 Contact: Ken Mitchell (Director)	•	•	•	•			
John May School of Business Speaking and Communication Administrative Offices Bovinger Lodge Ongar Essex CM5 0LT Telephone: 0378 75000 Contact: Courses Secretary	•	•	•				•
Melrose Film Productions Ltd 8–12 Old Queen Street London SW1H 9HP Telephone: 01-222 1744 Telex: 917944 IMELDN G Contact: Debbie Mules	•		•	•			
Middle Aston House Training and Conference Centre Middle Aston Oxford OX5 3PT Telephone: 0869 40361 Contact: Mr Brian Box	•	•	•	•			

	talks and speeches	closed-circuit tv	visual aids	effective writing	the press	radio	television
Missenden Abbey Management Centre Great Missenden Bucks HP16 0BD Telephone: 02406 6811 Contact: Joyce Jackson	●	●					
Monadnock International Ltd 2 The Chapel Royal Victoria Patriotic Building Fitzhugh Grove London SW18 3SX Telephone: 01-871 2546 Telex: 299180 MONINT G Contact: E C Botti	●	●	●	●	●	●	●
MSS Services Ltd 31A Chapel Road Worthing West Sussex BN11 1EG Telephone: 0903 34755/6 Telex: 87323 Contact: Marcia Gay	●	●	●	●			
O.M.L. Associates Willowbrook Valley Hill Nr Wells Somerset BA5 1PA Telephone: 0749 76103 Contact: Barry Peel	●						
Oral Communication Services 101 Alcester Road Hollywood Nr Birmingham B47 5NR Telephone: 021-430 6506 Contact: Mr Leslie Dunn (Director)	●			●	●	●	●

	talks and speeches	closed-circuit tv	visual aids	effective writing	the press	radio	television
OTMA Ltd Victoria House Southampton Row London WC1B 4DH Telephone: 01-405 4730 Telex: 21792 Contact: Peter Whyborn (Director)	●	●	●				
PACE (Performance & Communication Enterprises) Ltd Cedar Court 9–11 Fairmile Henley-on-Thames Oxon RG9 2JR Telephone: 0491 57961 Telex: 846068 CEDAR Contact: David Gaster or Roy Johnson	●	●		●			
Partners in Training Ltd Cromwell House 13 Ogleforth York YO1 2JG Telephone: 0904 56472 Telex: 57854 SLS 1G Contact: Barry Stainthorp (Director)	●	●		●			
P.E.R.A Nottingham Road Melton Mowbray Leicestershire LE13 0PB Telephone: 0664 501501 Telex: 34684 PERAMM G Contact: M J Mayes (Head of Training)	●	●	●	●			
Peterborough Software (UK) Ltd Thorpe Park Peterborough PE3 6JY Telephone: 0733 41010 Telex: 32307 Contact: Roger Wentworth	●	●	●	●			

	talks and speeches	closed-circuit tv	visual aids	effective writing	the press	radio	television
Pointers Group 7 Pointers Back Lane Ham Richmond Surrey TW10 7HQ Telephone: 01-948 4423/01-876 0984 Contact: Helen Taylor or Pamela Nottidge	•		•	•	•	•	•
Profact Consulting & Planning Ltd 64 Tremaine Road London SE20 7TZ Telephone: 01-778 4670 Telex: 94640 C WEASYG Contact: Steve Kennett	•	•	•				
Reading College of Technology Kings Road Reading RG1 4HJ Telephone: 0734 583501 Ext 145 Contact: Mrs Joan van Emden	•		•				
Reed Business Publishing Ltd Quadrant House The Quadrant Sutton Surrey SM1 5AS Telephone: 01-661 3500 Telex: 892084 BISPRS G Contact: Mr J Humphries (01-661 3979)	•	•	•			•	•
Roffey Park Management College Forest Road Horsham West Sussex RH12 4TD Telephone: 029 383 644 Contact: Mike Hallworth	•	•	•				
Royal Institute of Public Administration 3 Birdcage Walk London SW1H 9JH Telephone: 01-222 2248 Contact: Jane Cragg	•	•		•			

	talks and speeches	closed-circuit tv	visual aids	effective writing	the press	radio	television
Tim Russell 112 Defoe House Barbican London EC2 Telephone: 01-638 5357 Telex: 877830 SAKVIL G Contact: Tim Russell	●	●	●				
Scottish Business School 79 West George Street Glasgow G2 1EU Telephone: 041-221 3124 Contract: Mr W Drummond	●		●	●	●	●	●
The Scottish Council for Educational Technology (SCET) Dowanhill 74 Victoria Crescent Road Glasgow G12 9JN Telephone: 041-334 9314 Contact: George Paton (Director)				●			●
Selsdon Park Management Centre 31 Pollards Hill North London SW16 4NJ Telephone: 01-764 5109 Telex: 945003 SELPAK G Contact: Frank Wrigglesworth	●			●			
Sigma Training Services Portway House 26 St Matthews Road Bristol BS6 5TT Telephone: 0272 422918 Contact: Richard Storey	●	●		●			
Skills With People Ltd 15 Liberia Road London N5 1JP Telephone: 01-359 2370 Contact: Caroline Bailey (Director)	●	●			●	●	●

	talks and speeches	closed-circuit tv	visual aids	effective writing	the press	radio	television
South Bucks & East Berks Training Group Ltd 2-6 Bath Road Slough Bucks SL1 3SB Telephone: 0753 77877 Telex: 848314 Contact: John Willetts	•	•	•	•			
Speakeasy 17 Clifton Road London N3 2AS Telephone: 01-346 2776 Contact: Cristina Stuart	•	•	•	•	•	•	•
Speechpower The Nugget Samarkand Close Camberley Surrey GU15 1DG Telephone: 0276 21756 Contact: Roger Bacon	•	•	•	•			
Sundridge Park Management Centre Plaistow Lane Bromley Kent BR1 3TP Telephone: 01-460 8585 Telex: 265871 Contact: N J E Dwelly	•	•	•				
TACK Training International TACK House 1-5 Longmoore Street London SW1V 1JJ Telephone 01-834 5001 Telex: 497367 Contact: Eric Pillinger	•	•	•	•			

	talks and speeches	closed-circuit tv	visual aids	effective writing	the press	radio	television
Television Interview Training Consultancy Ltd 40 Whitelands House King's Road London SW3 4QY Telephone: 01-730 6428 Contact: Miss Helen Patterson (Secretary)	•				•	•	•
Tweed Services Ltd Mariner House 157–163 High Street Southend-on-Sea Essex Telephone: 0702 331012 Fax: 0702 354268 Contact: R N Harvey	•		•				
Urwick Management Centre, Price Waterhouse Baylis House Stoke Poges Lane Slough SL13 Telephone: 0753 34111 Telex: 848146 Contact: Mrs Ruth Drahota (Course Administrator)	•	•					
Vibes Ltd 3 Victoria Road Brighton Sussex BN1 3FS Telephone: 0273 21310 Contact: John Barden	•	•	•	•			
Wadlow Grosvenor Presentation Training 19/20 Grosvenor Street London W1X 9FD Telephone: 01-409 1225 Telex: 297761 BT1EQ/G WADLOW Contact: Adrienne Reynolds	•	•	•	•	•	•	•
Walpole Training & Development Ltd 61–63 St John Street London EC1M 4AN Telephone: 01-253 2340 Contact: Administrative Manager	•		•	•			

INDEX